EXPLORER OF THE UNCONSCIOUS:

Sigmund Freud

EXPLORER OF THE UNCONSCIOUS:

Sigmund Freud

By Adrien Stoutenburg and Laura Nelson Baker

CHARLES SCRIBNER'S SONS   NEW YORK

A–1.65[V]

The acknowledgments for *Explorer of the Unconscious: Sigmund Freud* appear on page 193.

Printed in the United States of America
Library of Congress Catalog Card Number 65-14772

To Kingsley D. Holman
Attorney at Law, Bloomington,
Minnesota, this book is
affectionately dedicated.

EXPLORER OF THE UNCONSCIOUS:

Sigmund Freud

CHAPTER 1

The street lamps had not yet been lighted, and the remaining daylight had a magic quality. In the restaurant in Vienna's beautiful park, the Prater, people sat at tables talking and relaxing, watching the hills surrounding the city turn violet-colored.

At one table sat a merchant, Jakob Freud and his wife, with their twelve-year-old son, Sigmund. Although the boy ate his apfelstrudel hungrily, his gaze flicked back and forth across the scene, observing the people, the building and the band of musicians assembling nearby, with interest.

Amalie Freud's attention centered chiefly on Sigmund. She was a young woman, much younger than her husband who had been married before, and Sigmund was the first-born of her seven children. She had reason to be proud of him for his handsomeness and his keen intelligence, but her devotion tended to be extreme. Nothing was too good for him, she believed, and although she loved her other offspring, Sigmund came first in her thoughts and plans. He was her "golden Sigi" even though his hair was blacker than his father's, his eyes darker than her own.

"There's the poet over there," Sigmund spoke up as the lamps began to flicker into life. He watched the lean man who was wandering from table to table, singing verses for whatever fee the patrons cared to give him. "I could make up rhymes as easily as he can."

"But perhaps he can't boast as well as you," Jakob Freud said. Jakob folded his napkin and leaned back. He was a robust man of fifty-two, with a wide, high forehead, fine eyebrows, a neatly trimmed beard, and sensitive looking hands. Like Amalie he was proud of Sigmund but his devotion could not be as unreserved as hers since he not only had two other, full-grown sons, Emmanuel and Philipp, but was a grandfather as well. Amalie had been only twenty years old when he had married her in 1855, after his first wife's death. Sigmund had been born on May 6, 1856. He was followed by another son, Julius, who died in infancy. Next had come five daughters, and then another boy Alex, now two years old. Looking at Sigmund, Jakob thought how much he resembled Amalie, though the wide, high forehead was his own, and of how close the two were. She spoiled him, no doubt of that. He himself was no strict patriarch though one thing he demanded and received from all his children was respect. He turned to Sigmund and said, "Ask the poet to come to our table."

Sigmund made his way toward the hired minstrel. The band started playing loudly and the sound struck his ears as unpleasantly as the sound of the piano at home when his oldest sister, Anna, had been trying to learn to play. He was not fond of most music; worse, her stumbling notes had distracted him so from his studies that he had complained until the piano was sold. It had not been fair to Anna, perhaps, but study was the important thing; both his father and mother had agreed.

When Sigmund led the poet to the Freud table, the minstrel bowed to Jakob and Amalie and said, "With your permission, before you provide a subject for me to put into my humble verses, I'd like to compose a few lines in praise of your handsome son."

Jakob glanced at Sigmund. Such flattery would turn the boy's head, although this was not the first time that he had been singled out for it or even for predictions of future greatness. He had been born in a caul, supposedly a sign that he was destined for high achievements. An old woman in a pastry shop had predicted fame for the boy, too, which had added to Amalie's determination to give Sigmund every opportunity to realize his talents. Talents Sigmund had, Jakob had to amit, and an exceptional ability to learn. He had gone into Sperl Gymnasium a year earlier than most boys, and almost at once he had risen to the top of his class.

Jakob nodded assent to the poet and sat back, both amusement and skepticism in his expression. Sigmund took his place quietly in his own chair.

"The boy will become a minister of state," the poet chanted in rhyme. "He will bring fame and honor to the family. He will be known all over Austria, for he has not only the fire of intelligence but he has also the dignity of a young king."

"That is enough glory for now," Jakob cut in, seeing the flush of excitement on his son's face, and the glow in Amalie's. A minister. It was not impossible. In earlier days a cabinet minister had to come from the nobility but now it was possible for a person from the middle classes to rise to such a high post. "Let us have some verses to our Vienna twilight."

The poet obliged. When he was through Jakob paid him for his efforts and the Freuds left.

As they walked along the tree-lined path leading out of the park, Amalie talked animatedly about the poet's prophesies and of the glorious day when her Sigi would be a leader in the Congress. She herself would sit in the front row and lead the applause.

Sigmund walked silently between his parents. Although he knew that he should not take the minstrel's words seriously, it was tempting to do so. The right choice of profession was extremely important. Perhaps he should devote himself to the study of law rather than to literature or science as he had considered doing. He put his thoughts into words as the three reached the point at which the Prater Strasse intersected their own street, the Kaiser Josefstrasse.

"It's fine to dream, Sigmund," Jakob said, "but you must

remember that you are a Jew. Things are a little better for us now but the humiliations and prejudice remain."

He did not need his father to remind him that he was a Jew, Sigmund thought, even though there had never been any emphasis on orthodox Hebrew religion in the family, since his father was a freethinker. It made no difference. Like most persons with a Jewish background in Vienna and elsewhere, he had been subjected to slurs, contempt and gestures of hostility by many gentiles from the beginning of his school days. And like the majority of Jews he was extremely sensitive to all expressions of anti-Semitism. Also, he had learned enough of history to know how often Jews had been persecuted over the centuries. Austrian Jews had been granted equality of rights last year, 1867, but the equality existed largely on paper. Even so, many Jews were pushing ahead into fields that had been closed to them before.

Sigmund watched a carriage go by, the horse's coat shining under the lamps which seemed so much brighter than the distant, faint stars. "Jews will have to fight for their rights like everybody else," he declared.

"That is easy to say," Jakob replied. He swung his walking stick against the stone wall of a garden. It made a sound like running pebbles. "Sometimes it is more sensible to go one's way peacefully. When I was a young man, I was walking one Saturday along the street in the village where you were born; I was well-dressed, with a new fur cap on my head. Up comes a Christian who knocks my cap into the mud and shouts, 'Jew, get off the pavement!' "

"And what did you do?" Sigmund looked at his father expectantly.

Jakob shrugged. "I went into the street and picked up the cap."

Sigmund felt shock and deep disillusion. He turned his face away, biting his lip. How could his father, who had always seemed so strong, have given in without a fight or even a protest? He felt his pride shrivel.

His mother, always perceptive of his moods, put her hand on his shoulder and said something gay to try to distract him from his somberness. He shook her hand away and ran ahead through the gathering darkness. In contrast to his father he thought of his heroes, the powerful military leaders such as Alexander the Great and Hannibal. Hannibal's father had made him swear before the household altar eternal vengeance against the Roman enemy. How different that was from the attitude his own father had just revealed.

A bat swooped past his face and he marveled at the precision of its flight even as his deeper thoughts still revolved around the shock he felt over his father's confession.

He reached the door of the family flat well ahead of his parents. All of his sisters were in the living room: Anna, Rosa, Marie, Adolfine and Paula. Anna was holding baby Alexander in her lap. Sigmund took the baby from her, accusing with pretended severity:

"How is he going to walk if you keep holding him all the time?"

Anna said, "Just because you chose his name doesn't mean you know everything, Sigi."

"Perhaps I will know everything someday," Sigmund boasted, swinging his brother up in his arms. He told the girls of the wandering poet's prophesy, making a face to imply that he didn't really believe it, but he felt satisfaction when they looked properly impressed. He set Alex down, thinking that this namesake of Alexander the Great was not apt to conquer any kingdoms very soon. Anyhow, he had his own kingdom to conquer tonight, twenty pages of Greek.

He went toward his room, which was called a "cabinet." Ordinarily he ate his evening meals there so as to lose no time from his studies. Anna picked Alexander up again, admonishing the other girls to be quiet because Sigmund was going to study.

Sigmund walked into his room. Long and narrow though it was, containing only a bed, a chair, bookshelves and his desk, it was entirely his. No one else in the family had a private room. And only he had an oil lamp to himself; the other bedrooms had candles. He hung up his suit jacket; it was his only good one and must not be spattered by ink from his pen.

As he sat down and pulled a book toward him, he heard his parents arrive. The image of his father picking up his cap from the gutter loomed between him and the Greek letters on the book's pages. He forced it away, rested his forehead on his fists, and made himself concentrate on the task before him.

He had studied for an hour when there was a knock at his door. Sigmund started and asked sharply who was there.

His father stepped into the room. The gray in his beard showed up in the lamplight. He pulled a small, leather-covered book from his pocket and held it out.

Sigmund saw the author's name. Goethe. He opened the book eagerly, then looked at his father in surprise. Although there were books in the house, they were a luxury, for there was seldom enough money for more than practical necessities.

"There's a small stain on the cover. I got it cheap," Jakob said. He remained looking intently at Sigmund, waiting for Sigmund to speak.

"It's a wonderful present, Papa," Sigmund said, regretting the sharpness in his voice before.

When his father left, Sigmund sat down with the small book and read softly to himself. "Seele des Menschen, Wie gleichst du dem Wasser. Schnicksal des Menschen, Wie gleichst du dem Wind!" Spring of man, how like water you are. Destiny of man, how like the wind!

A night breeze tapped the roof. Sigmund leaned his chin on his hands, thinking of the poet at the Prater and of his father again. It was his father who had been his first teacher, and it was thanks to his father's training that he had learned to apply his mind to his studies so well. He remembered hearing his father boast to a friend, "At age seven, my son was reading the Bible! At eight, Shakespeare, in English. His little toe is cleverer than my head. But for all that, he would never dare to contradict me."

Sigmund pushed his heavy hair back from his forehead. Now, as before, he felt confused when thinking about his relationship to his father. Why shouldn't Papa be contradicted as well as Mama? Because he was the man of the household? He himself would be a man soon. And his father was certainly not all wise or all powerful; that had been proven by the anecdote he had told tonight. But he was a good companion. Sigmund fingered the Goethe book's cover, remembering all the walks he and his father had taken around the city, his father telling him the history of the places they passed. Often he would tell Jewish jokes and they would laugh together.

Sigmund pulled his Greek study book toward him again, impatient with his own idle thoughts. Every minute should be spent in improving himself. Only by work could one become a cabinet minister or a famous general, especially when there was the obstacle of being a Jew. His pride welled up again, reinforcing his determination, and he became oblivious to everything except his effort to understand what was on the page before him.

CHAPTER 2

Sigmund Freud, aged sixteen, stood in his cabinet, but for once, he was not studying. He was looking into the mirror which reflected his slim figure and intensely dark eyes. He touched a scar on his chin briefly. It had been there since he was two years old when he had had a violent fall. He turned his concentration on fixing his tie properly. Neatness was important, no matter how inexpensive one's clothes might be, and he was especially eager to make a good impression when he arrived at his birthplace, Freiberg, where he was going for a brief visit.

He heard a questioning voice behind him and turned to see Alexander, now six years old. Alexander wanted to know if he could play with the wooden soldiers Sigmund had collected over the years.

Sigmund went toward the shelf where the collection was kept in a box. He took one of the soldiers out and looked at it reflectively. On the toy's back was a label he had once pasted there. Andre Masséna, it said. A general under Napoleon Bonaparte, supposedly a Jew. Masséna had been his favorite of all Napoleon's marshalls. Now the days of his military fervor had passed, though only two years ago he had still been excited over military figures and campaigns. That had been when the Franco-Prussian War broke out in July of 1870. He remembered how he had made Anna and Rosa come into his room to hear him describe the battles, demonstrating the position of the opposing armies by flags which he moved across a map of Europe.

He passed the miniature soldiers on to Alex, each figure wearing a name label on the back. Hannibal, Alexander the Great, Oliver Cromwell . . .

His mother appeared in the doorway. She looked at him searchingly but approvingly. He was going to be the guest of old friends of the family in Freiberg, Herr and Frau Fluss, and Amalie was concerned that he should appear at his best.

The Flusses, Sigmund thought, would have to take him as he was, including their daughter Gisela. She was about his own age and had been his playmate when he was small. He mentioned Gisela, with a smile, to his mother.

"You are too young to be thinking of frauleins!" she said with uncustomary reproof in her voice. "You are to go to school many years and become somebody important."

Sigmund tightened a strap on his suitcase. "Perhaps a person has to be important in himself before he can seem so to others."

"And you are, mein goldener Sigi. You are a genius."

"One is not a genius; one has genius." He spoke as if he were the teacher, his mother a pupil.

His mother shook her head, not in disapproval but in wonder. At moments Sigmund talked like someone at least twenty years older than he was. And how quickly his moods varied, from high humor to a brooding introspection. Sometimes he spoke sharply, from exasperation, or out of the pain of the headaches which occasionally afflicted him. There seemed to be no cause for these unless it was his own emotional intensity. At other times, no one could be gayer or more full of humor, or have a keener wit to parry Jakob's. Whatever else he was, he was never unkind.

She left, taking Alex with her, as it was time for his bath. Reluctantly, Alex left the armies he had been marching on his brother's desk, letting himself be propelled in the direction of the wooden tub which had been filled by hired carriers who delivered water to the house.

Sigmund finished his packing and strolled into the living room. The wall clock showed that there were still three hours before the train to Freiberg was due to leave, plenty of time for his father to come and take him to the bahnhof. Yet Sigmund felt a mounting tension of the kind he experienced whenever he took a train trip, together with a dull headache.

Ridiculous, he told himself, but he had to find a way to ease his nervousness. There would be time to walk to the Belvedere museum and prowl around among the antiquities there. The sight of ancient coins, mummies and statues always thrilled and relaxed him at the same time. Only, today he did not feel that even the calmness of the museum would help. It would be better to walk, or to talk to someone. He would drop in on his friend, Silberstein, he decided; he and his friend had not practiced their Spanish conversations for a week or more now.

He called at Silberstein's house and the two went off for a short ramble, but they did not speak much Spanish. Sigmund was too distracted by his trip. The whole idea of travel appealed to him, he said, but he always grew nervous before starting out, especially if a train were involved. He had not made many journeys, but the experience was always the same. Why this was he didn't know, he told Silberstein when the latter looked perplexed. The only clue he had was that he remembered vividly his first train journey when he was only three years old. At that time his father had moved from Freiberg because his business in textile manufacture there had been on the downgrade, partly as the result of animosity toward the Jews. On the way to Leipzig, where the family was to settle for a year before moving on to Vienna, Sigmund had seen gas jets for the first time as the train went through Breslau. He had felt a strange terror at the sight of the flames shooting into the air.

"I can still see them skewering up like the torches of hell," he told his companion.

Silberstein laughed. "Don't tell me you believe in hell."

"No, but my nurse in Freiberg did, and she stuffed me full of tales of souls writhing in eternal fire."

"Why should something so long past bother you now?"

Sigmund shook his head, unable to answer.

Two hours later, he was on his way to Freiberg, Moravia. As the train reached open country, Sigmund struggled to remember what his life had been like in those very early years in Freiberg. Emmanuel and Philipp, his two half-brothers had lived there then, too, and Emmanuel's little son, John. John had been a year older than Sigmund, and yet Sigmund was his uncle. Even now it was confusing to think of how he could have a nephew a year older than himself. In many ways, John had been the most important individual in his life in those infant years. They had played together and fought together; John, a year older and stronger, had been both tyrant and friend. In the fights Sigmund had fought back strenuously, for it was not in his nature to give in. One of the strangest parts of the experience, for Sigmund, was that the older boy should call Jakob "grandfather." Even stranger was the fact that Philipp and his own mother Amalie, who were of the same age, should not sleep in the same bed together. As it was, it was his father Jakob who paired off with his young mother, though it seemed more logical to the child Sigmund that his father and the old nurse, his Nannie, should be the ones to share the same bedroom.

Sigmund stared through the train's dusty window. It had all been very puzzling and still was. He could understand the family relationships now, logically, but the emotional confusion remained. Emmanuel, Philipp and John lived in England now, Emmanuel working in the textile business in Manchester. He would go there to visit them sometime; his father had promised. In his imagination he pretended that he was watching a green English countryside beyond the windows, breathing the air of a society where Jews were not persecuted as in Austria—and felt envious of his father's other two sons. Why his father had not moved there too he did not know. Perhaps his father was too timid or too old; he was nephew John's grossvater, after all, with gray hairs beneath his underlip.

Sigmund pulled a book of essays from his luggage and forced himself to study it. What good did it do to dig into wishes or the past or to blame his father for what could not be helped?

Freiberg came in view at last, a small, peaceful looking village ringed by forests and meadows. On the railway platform stood a genial, smiling Herr Fluss with his three sons, Emil, Richard and Alfred. They greeted Sigmund and escorted him to a carriage. Even before they reached it, Sigmund, conscientious about the practical aspects of his journey, handed Herr Fluss the business papers and messages his father had entrusted to him.

Fluss directed the driver of the carriage to travel down the Annaberger Strasse so that Sigmund could see his old home. When the carriage reached 117 Schlossergasse, where Sigmund had been born, Sigmund shook his head wonderingly. Though he had lived there for the first years of his life, the house looked totally unfamiliar. How strange and fickle memory was.

The voices of Fluss's sons broke in upon his thoughts as the carriage went on, questioning him about his life in Vienna and his plans for what he would do after his graduation from high school. Sigmund told them that he had not decided yet, but that possibly he might study law.

The carriage wheels rattled to a stop in front of a house which looked warm and welcoming because of the lights shining through the windows.

"Here we are," Herr Fluss said. While his sons took Sigmund's baggage, he steered his visitor ahead of him, across the yard and into the Fluss living room. There stood a smiling Frau Fluss and behind her a slender, pretty, dark-haired girl.

Gisela, Sigmund realized, even before they were formally introduced. He was normally shy at meeting strangers; he felt even more so now as he bowed awkwardly and murmured a greeting. His heart was knocking very strangely; no girl had ever affected him quite this way before. Perhaps it was because he had so little time for them outside his studies. Or perhaps he had not met the right girl until now. Could it be true, as some of his friends at the Gymnasium said, that one could fall in love at first sight?

By the time he had been in the Fluss household for a day, Sigmund concluded that he had indeed fallen in love and he was not sure that he liked the emotion. If Gisela looked at him and smiled shyly, his hopes flared to a pitch that was almost painful. If she frowned or ignored him, he felt abjectly miserable. Actually, he saw little of her. She was busy with her own affairs and seldom joined Sigmund and her brothers in their excursions to the woods, or to the mines which had been developed centuries before. When he did meet her or sat across from her at meals, he was tongue-tied and said little.

Only a few days after his arrival in Freiberg, Gisela left to go back to a school she was attending in another town. Sigmund felt more desolate than he could have believed was possible. Disconsolate, he wandered about silently, scarcely able to think of anything but Gisela. Dared he write to her? Would she answer? He derided himself for his failure to make her know how he felt. His mind had been full of ardent speeches but he had stammered and bumbled like an ignorant bumpkin. How different it might have been if he had grown up here in Freiberg, close to Gisela, or even if he could remain. She could not be off to school forever. But, because his father had decided to move to Vienna, the opportunity had been lost. He thought longingly of how much happier matters would have turned out had they all stayed in Freiberg; he would have followed his father in the textile business, married Gisela Fluss, raised a family and been satisfied on a humble scale.

But now Gisela was gone and there was little chance that he would see her again, let alone woo her. It was, he decided irrationally, all his father's fault.

Some of his bitterness came out during conversations with Emil, to whom he had taken a liking. Emil was lucky to live in Freiberg; Vienna was hostile and barbarous, for all the gaiety on the surface and its claims to culture, Sigmund said.

During one of these talks the chimes of Freiberg's St.

Mary's church rang out. "It's not so easy here, either, Sigmund," said Emil, inclining his head toward the sound. "Freiberg's largely Catholic; we Jews are very much of a minority, and there aren't the educational opportunities that you have in Vienna."

"Everybody's a minority when it comes to that," Sigmund answered, refusing to be consoled even though he knew that what Emil said was true. "A minority of one."

On his way back to Vienna, Sigmund once again sat staring through the train window trying to sort out his muddled thoughts and emotions. He still felt an ache of longing when he thought of Gisela, though perhaps it was not quite as intense as right after her departure. Time healed, people said. Perhaps. He could only hope so. The violent emotion he had felt over Gisela was a distraction to his work, which should come first. His family was sacrificing much to give him an education; the only way he could repay them was by distinguishing himself in his studies and his life.

By the time the train rolled into the Vienna station Freud felt that he had his emotions and ambitions firmly in hand once more. He would study harder than ever, not only for his parents' sake but for his own. Always he had had an intense desire to understand the many riddles of the world and a need to contribute something to their solution. At the same time, he realized that his mind often went off into dreamy speculations and cloudy abstractions in a way that could lead him far from the realms of useful fact. He would ruthlessly check that tendency in himself, he resolved, and try to counter it by concentrating on what was proven and scientific. Which, he thought ruefully, could not include Gisela Fluss or any other fraulein, or at least not for a long time to come.

In June of the following year, 1873, Sigmund Freud took his final examinations at the Gymnasium. In the course of these he submitted a paper he had written, called "Considerations Involved in a Choice of a Profession." His professor complimented him on his writing style.

Sigmund had written the paper shortly after hearing a public reading of an essay by Goethe on nature, an occasion which had stirred him deeply. A faithful study of nature, said Goethe, would provide an answer to all secrets.

Science, especially biology, Sigmund considered, would be the searcher's best tool. Charles Darwin's startling theories on the evolution of man pointed the way toward a new understanding of the world.

In the midst of his examinations Sigmund wrote to Emil Fluss. He jokingly told Emil of the professor's praise of his paper, saying that Emil probably had not been previously aware that he had been receiving letters from a literary stylist. In a more serious vein, he took Emil to task. "You take my 'worries about the future' too lightly. People who fear nothing but mediocrity, you say are safe. Safe from what? I ask. Surely not safe and secure from being mediocre."

There was nothing mediocre about Sigmund's scholastic achievements; he graduated from Sperl Gymnasium with the top honors, summa cum laude. He had a natural gift for languages, including Latin, Greek and English, plus the Italian and Spanish which he had taught himself. He had grown up learning Hebrew. Outside his regular studies he read widely, both fact and fiction, and had time left over to teach his sisters.

His boyish dream of becoming a minister of state was as dead as his dreams of being a general, since the reality was that a Viennese Jew could scarcely hope for such roles. He was limited to finding a life for himself in business or industry, law or medicine.

Business did not appeal to him though he knew that his father at times, apprehensive that his intellectual pursuits might not lead him to a stable income, wished that he might direct his abilities that way. Nor had he ever cared for medicine and playing the "doctor game." However, one did not have to be a doctor to pursue science, and certainly science was the field that offered to expand man's knowledge of the universe and even of himself. For his own self, scientific study would be a helpful discipline.

When Sigmund Freud entered the University of Vienna in the fall of 1873 he was still uncertain as to what he would specialize in, but he continued to cling to the need of studying "fact." In his first semester he signed up for twelve lectures in anatomy, six in chemistry and practical work in both subjects, and so launched himself as a medical student.

But the dreamy part of his nature continued to exert a strong pull so that he found it difficult at first to feel any great enthusiasm for his scientific studies. He kept at them, nevertheless, expanding his courses to include botany, microscopy, mineralogy, biology and Darwinism.

Jakob Freud, watching his son, felt increasing doubt. Such studies would not lead to a living very soon, and bad times had wiped out most of his own savings. Emmanuel and Philipp were doing well for their families in England and Emmanuel's daughter, Pauline, was the right age to make Sigmund a steady, sensible wife. Sigmund could do worse than to follow his half-brothers' pattern.

In 1875, when Sigmund was nineteen, Jakob took him on the long-promised journey to England. Whatever Sigmund thought of Manchester, or Pauline, and the life there, he did not stay but returned with his father to Vienna. Apparently the textile business had no appeal for him for he went back with fresh determination to his microscope, dissecting fishes and eels, disciplining himself with increased firmness.

Amalie Freud watched, like her husband, but there was no doubt in her mind. Her Sigi, her golden one, was destined for greatness even though he came home with the scent of lowly crayfish on his fingers, or talked of nothing more magnificent than the spinal cord of a peculiar kind of fish.

When he told her that he was branching out into original research in zoology and had been given a grant to go to Trieste to study at an experimental station there, she was exuberant. Fame would surely come ultimately as his reward.

Sigmund understood the rigors of research better than his mother. Even though fame might result, it would not necessarily mean riches.

His mother tapped her forehead. "The fortune is up here."

Sigmund nodded and pressed his own forehead with his fingertips, feeling the first dull signs of a migraine headache beginning there. He was too keyed up over the Trieste trip, he decided; or perhaps he had been peering through his microscope too long. "Yes, Mama," he said. Though he had faith in himself, a knowledge of all that there was to learn made him humble. "Only, I wish that the Almighty had given me a greater fortune to spend."

CHAPTER 3

Sigmund Freud slipped cautiously through the door to the lecture room at the Brücke Institute of Physiology, hoping his tardiness would not be noticed. He was almost to his chair when the lecturer's voice, with its Prussian accent, stopped. The professor fixed Freud with his cold blue eyes.

Freud flinched under the doctor's accusing gaze. No one was more demanding than Brücke; yet no one was more kind toward a student who proved his ability. In fact, it was only since he had been accepted at the Institute that Sigmund Freud had felt true satisfaction in his scientific researches. He was twenty years old, a kind of research scholar singled out for attention by Brücke who was an authority in a field called physical physiology. The body behaved as it did, according to Brücke, because of masses, charges and currents of energy within it. In the nervous system waves of excitement or energy built up, overflowed and spread throughout the nerve structures. Everything in nature, including man, functioned in accordance with predetermined laws which, with patience and work, could be discovered.

Now, at the moment, Brücke was talking about more specific problems, the structure of the nerve cells of some of the lower animals. Freud, adjusting his microscope over a slide holding the cells of a fish, wondered: how could truth be here in these shiny particles? But if not here, where else? If he did not believe that through such research fundamental answers could be found, his whole summer in Trieste studying the reproductive organs of eels had been wasted.

Freud concentrated on Brücke's lecture. Brücke and his two assistants, Ernst von Fleischl-Marxow and Sigmund Exner, were men he respected more than any he had met before. But he especially admired Brücke with his dedication to observable truth. He was, Freud felt, someone to model his life after.

After the lecture he sought out Fleischl-Marxow. Fleischl, though he was ten years older than Freud, was interested in the same tormenting intellectual questions. Also, he was handsome, enthusiastic about science and had a personal charm which drew Freud toward him.

Freud found the assistant in one of the crowded cubicles that served as a laboratory. Fleischl turned from his examination of a frog's brain to greet Sigmund with a smile. At once they began talking of their various researches, and then Freud mentioned his fear that Brücke was angry at him for his having been unavoidably late for the lecture.

"He'll forgive you. You can't help but know that he's very interested in you and eager for you to succeed. He says that in your work on the histology of nerve cells you've made a major discovery and are on the road to new ones."

Freud made a modest rejoinder, trying to conceal his satisfaction in hearing of Brücke's praise. He, himself, knew that his discovery that the cells of the nervous system of the lower animals were similar to those of the higher, was important, for it closed the gap between different forms of life which had formerly been presumed to exist; but it was good to be reassured by someone he respected so much. Also, Brücke had told him that he was going to present Freud's paper on the subject to the Academy of Sciences of Vienna. He had learned much from Brücke; the man seemed like a second father. The forty years difference in their age contributed to this feeling, Freud supposed; with Brücke he felt something of the trusting security he had felt toward his real father when he had been small.

A sudden expression of pain on Fleischl's face took Freud's thoughts from himself. He glanced toward Fleischl's right hand. There was only scar tissue where the thumb had once been. Five years ago, the assistant's thumb had become infected during an experiment he was making in pathological anatomy and had been amputated. Fleischl kept developing tumors on the nerves of the hand which required further operations. In spite of that, and almost constant pain, the young man continued to perform feats of amazing skill and delicacy in the laboratories.

At Freud's concerned, questioning look, Fleischl rubbed his disfigured hand. "Only a twinge. Everyone suffers something. Let's step out of this clammy basement and get some fresh air."

Outside Freud lighted a cigar, puffing the blue smoke onto the summer breeze. Perhaps it was true that everyone must suffer, but it seemed unfair that someone with as promising a career as Fleischl should have to endure so much. No religion that he had ever known, including the Hebrew faith, had answered the question of unnecessary suffering to his satisfaction. Healing and release appeared to be the products of science, not theology.

Freud continued his researches at the Institute with increasing vigor. During the summer months of 1879 and 1880, he did further work on the nerve cells of lower animals, coming close to describing the neurone theory which is today taught in all physiology courses: a nerve cell and its nerve fibers form a unit which makes all nervous activity possible. Also at this period, Freud began to serve his year's term of military service. At the time, in Austria, there was very little actual military training for such recruits. Medical students were permitted to live at home and were required to stand about in attendance at hospitals with only routine tasks to perform. Freud used his spare time at the hospital to translate a book by John Stuart Mill into German, to relieve the monotony and to make some extra money.

Lack of money was a harassing problem. He could not remain dependent on his father forever, and he faced the fact that whether he really wished to practice medicine or not, he must take the examinations for a Doctor of Medicine degree. He took the first ones on June 9, 1880, with his friend Fleischl-Marxow as examiner, in chemistry, botany, and zoology. He was graded "Excellent" in these. He did not do so well, however, in general medicine under a different examiner, so he went back to Brücke's laboratory for another ten months. On March 30, 1881, he passed his final examinations. The next day he took part in the graduation ceremonies and received his degree.

The diploma meant little to him except that it proved he had not been loafing in his studies, and was a help toward future advancement. He still did not wish to be a physician, preferring to continue laboratory research with the hope that eventually he might become a teacher or an Assistant Professor. Long ago, when he had committed some childish mischief one day, his father had said in disgust, "That boy will never amount to anything!" He would prove his father wrong.

Freud went back to continue research at the Physiological Institute, convinced that there, by studying all branches of biology, he could win success. Before long he achieved a comparatively minor position of Demonstrator at the Institute, and did some teaching on his own, but generally the year seemed to him gloomy and unrewarding.

He still lived at home, spending long hours studying in his cabinet, his main recreation being that of joining the members of his "bund," a band of mutual friends, for walks, the theatre, conversations or card games. Emil and Richard Fluss were now members of the bund, for the Fluss family had moved to Vienna. As for Gisela, the emotions she had roused in Freud years before had flickered out. Other emotions contended in him now, and intellectual ferment. Moods of depression and exultation alternated, often with no apparent cause. What were the springs of such moods and how could one learn better how to cope with them? A sense of frustra-tion over his own ignorance often drove him to take long, roving, mind-searching walks about the city. He was a tireless walker and a good swimmer. Physical activity seemed to ease the activity of his mind. Many a night Freud would pause at the bridge which spanned the Danube Canal near his home, staring down into night-darkened water. Nerve cells might gleam under the microscope, but what about man's inner self? How could one peel back the spongy layers of man's mind to lay thought bare? If everything worked by cause and effect, then it should be possible to find the cause of what people called "blind" emotions.

During this period of groping Freud became increasingly friendly with a man who was to be one of his chief benefactors, an Austrian physician, Josef Breuer. Breuer was a tall, handsome man with a golden-red beard, some fourteen years older than Freud. Freud said that to talk to Breuer was like "sitting in the sun." Although Breuer belonged to the same school of physiology as Brücke, he too had stared into the dark waters of man's mind. In Freud he found a person he could talk to. Freud poured his own thoughts out to the highly successful physician. He was rewarded both by Breuer's giving him his own more extensive scientific experience and by financial loans. For many years Breuer helped Freud over difficult periods where money was lacking, so that eventually Freud owed the doctor as much in *gulden* as in scientific knowledge.

After stimulating discussions with Breuer, Freud went back faithfully to his work at the Institute. In due time he might, with luck, hold the post of his beloved professor, Ernst Brücke, although it would be a long, long wait as Fleischl and Exner, both young, were ahead of him.

Among other friends of Freud at this time was Eli Bernays, a member of Freud's bund. Eli was a young man who had come from Hamburg, the grandson of a famous German rabbi, and he had developed a strong romantic attachment toward Freud's sister Anna. Another bund member was Ignaz Schönberg who was betrothed to Eli's sister Minna.

Even though Eli was the sole support of his widowed mother and his sisters, he generally managed to have more money than most of the other members in the bund, thanks to his talent for business. One night after Ignaz Schönberg's engagement to Minna had been announced, Eli suggested that the group celebrate the occasion at a cafe more expensive than the one usually chosen.

Freud went willingly, walking with his friends through the sharp December air toward the Kur Salon Restaurant in Vienna's city park. The Salon catered chiefly to tourists and wealthier Viennese. He glanced at his slightly threadbare coat, knowing that in spite of how carefully or neatly he dressed he appeared what he was, a poor, Jewish student. The thought did not dim his spirits, however, which were high. His sense of humor, too, was in good form so that his sallies and wit brought appreciative laughter from his comrades.

Only Ignaz Schönberg remained somewhat somber, though he regarded Freud with affection. He was a lean, frail young man, a brilliant scholar chiefly concerned with Sanskrit and ancient literature, and with his hopes for his marriage with Minna. He and Freud spent hours together discussing literature, philosophy and the arts. Now when Freud questioned him about his seeming melancholy, Ignaz confessed that he was brooding about the long wait necessary before he and Minna could be married, because of lack of money.

Eli Bernays, overhearing, said, "People should marry for love, not money. I tell both my sisters that. Telling my mother anything is a different matter. She has a mind of her own."

Freud had met the mother only briefly, the two Bernays sisters not at all, although Schönberg kept insisting that he must meet his beloved Minna. Frau Bernays, Freud had decided after his brief meeting with her, was a dominant personality who might be a problem to the sensitive, gentle Ignaz.

During the dinner and festivities, one of the group challenged Freud, "Isn't it about time that you lost your heart to some fraulein, Sigmund?"

"He's too in love with his studies," Eli said.

Freud countered their banter good-naturedly. Inwardly, he admitted that probably what Eli had said was true. There seemed to be no room for romance in his life, but at the same time he knew that he had a very ardent, passionate nature.

As the group of friends walked homeward toward the Leopoldstadt which was the Jewish section of the city, Richard Fluss exclaimed, "Look!" He pointed in the direction of the Schottenring where red flames spread against the sky.

The young men ran toward the flames, joined by other citizens of Vienna.

"It's the Ring Theatre!" voices shouted.

Even at a safe distance from the burning building Freud could feel heat searing his face. Beside him, Schönberg said, shuddering, "There are crowds of people still trapped inside, someone says, dying like gnats in a bonfire." His face looked pale in spite of the light of the flames. He coughed against the smoke, his hand pressing his side.

Freud felt concern for Ignaz' weak lungs and took his elbow, gently pushing him back through the throng. At the edge of the crowd he turned and looked again at the blazing inferno, feeling both horror and awe at the workings of fate. He had nearly purchased tickets to the performance at the theatre for this night to hear Offenbach conduct his "Tales of Hoffman."

The Ring Theatre burned to the ground, six hundred persons losing their lives in the fire. The date was December 2, 1881.

CHAPTER 4

It was Freud's custom when he brought friends home to take them back to his cabinet, shut the door and spend the time in intimate conversation. Freud had little time to spare for romantic thoughts. Preoccupied with his own pursuits, he failed to notice his sisters' eager interest in these male friends.

Rosa finally took Freud to task for not realizing that they had few opportunities to get to know young men outside their own small circle. Did he think she and the other girls were so ugly that he was ashamed to introduce them?

Freud felt apologetic, especially toward Rosa who was his favorite. He had been thoughtless, he admitted. His sisters did have to depend on finding satisfactory husbands in order to have future lives of their own. If they failed he was prepared to support them, however little he might earn.

"My friends are all very solemn fellows," he said by way of an excuse.

"Eli Bernays isn't," Marie said. "I've seen the smiles he casts in Anna's direction."

Anna looked up from her sewing. "Sigi doesn't give us a thought," she said sharply, "not as long as we're quiet and don't interfere with his work and read the kind of books he thinks we should."

Her voice jangled against his ears as unpleasantly as the notes of her piano had years before. He protested that she was being unfair, even though he knew there was some justice in her remark. The truth was that he had always resented his oldest sister a bit, if only because until her arrival he had been the center of his mother's world. Still, he was much too mature now to feel such jealousy; yet, perhaps some remnant of it lingered. Certainly he didn't have to question his position in the household. The whole family looked toward him as their main hope of achieving distinction or wealth. He went on toward his room, resolving to try to be more thoughtful of his sisters in the future.

One night in April, 1882, as Freud came into the flat, he heard a girl's light, joyful laugh. The sound drew him to the dining room where the family was still seated at the supper table.

There a girl sat peeling an apple and laughing at some anecdote Freud's father was telling her. She was a slim, somewhat pale girl, with glossy black hair parted in the middle and drawn straight back from her face in a kind of classical severity. Her eyes were large and filled with animation and seemed, at first glance, to be the color of emeralds. She was not beautiful, Freud thought, in a painter's or sculptor's sense of the word, yet "beautiful" was the only word for her that he could find.

"This is Martha Bernays," his mother said, then gestured to another girl at the table. "And her sister Minna."

Minna was younger and more robust, Freud saw, with a suggestion of aggressiveness that he decided might be part of her attraction for his friend Schönberg. Both sisters had a look of lively intelligence that they shared with their brother Eli, but it was Martha who attracted Freud most.

At his father's invitation Freud joined the group at the table, though he generally took his supper nearer the Institute. Amused, he noticed the look of surprise in his mother's eyes—and was there, also, a touch of apprehension? Perhaps she did not think he was old enough even yet to be interested in frauleins. Well, he wasn't greatly interested in frauleins, plural. But Martha Bernays was another matter. Why hadn't Eli insisted that he meet her before? He was almost prepared to believe that Eli had deliberately concealed her from him.

Later, in his room, he stood staring blankly at a copy of the American Declaration of Independence which Eli Bernays had once given him. All that he could see was Martha's face.

For the following three weeks Freud struggled to resist the attraction toward Martha which had flared up in him from almost his first glimpse of her. On the occasions when she appeared at the flat again he was rude and even pretended indifference. Nothing helped to subdue the violent emotion that he experienced whenever he saw her or thought of her. It was as if a dam had broken in him and all the passion and desire for love which he had denied for so long had burst through.

At the end of the three weeks Freud gave in. He was hopelessly in love with Eli's sister; there was nothing to do but court her and try to win her as his wife. Having set his heart on this, he proceeded to pursue her with all the determination and intensity that was his, which was a great deal. He began sending her a red rose every day, with his card and with a suitable motto in Latin, Spanish, English and German on each occasion. And now, each time they met, usually in the company of Frau Bernays or Minna, he exerted himself to try to win a smile from her or a glance that would indicate that his emotion was returned.

He alternated between hope and despair. On their first private talk together, in May, they walked down the Kahlenberg, her arm in his. He plucked a small spray of oak leaves and offered them. When Martha declined them, he interpreted this as a sign of rejection and vowed that he would hate oak trees forever. Like other serious young men of the day he kept a diary. In it he wondered whether he could ever mean a fraction as much to Martha as she did to him. For one thing, there appeared to be rivals on the scene, her cousin Max Mayer, for one. Fritz Wahle was another.

Freud's capacity for jealousy and self-torment was as great

as for love, and when he thought of the possibility of Martha's preferring someone else to him he suffered as deeply as if he had actually been betrayed.

But there were encouragements and joy, too. One day in early June as he and Martha walked through a garden, he found a double almond. According to Viennese custom, this called for an exchange of gifts. The next day Freud sent her a copy of *David Copperfield*. She, in turn, sent him a cake for him to "dissect," and a warm note of thanks for the book which she signed informally, "Martha."

From then on, the courtship proceeded rapidly, although it did not always go smoothly, thanks chiefly to Freud's tempestuous nature. Martha was sweet-tempered but she had a mind of her own and when Freud pressed her too far or made unreasonable demands she was quite capable of resisting him, and did.

Freud idealized Martha beyond all bounds of reality. He compared her to the princess in the fairy tale from whose lips roses and pearls fell whenever she spoke and yearned to call her "Princess." For the moment he would be happy if she would give him permission to address her as *"du,"* the German word for "you" which is used only between persons with close ties. Martha gave him permission and Freud was exultant.

One cloud remained—his poor financial condition. Marriage was out of the question without money to provide for a wife, home and family. Although romantic ardor had swept him off his feet, Freud had a healthy respect for money and was hard-headed enough to know that he could not propose without at least the promise of a more stable income. Then there was his responsibility toward his own family. His father was approaching seventy; soon he would be unable to carry on such business as he had. There was no one but himself for the family to rely on, Alexander being still too young to contribute much financially.

Working in the laboratories of the Institute, or taking long, striding walks by himself, Freud wrestled with his problem. The life of scholarly research which he desired would probably not provide an adequate income for years. Since he had his medical degree the logical step was to go into the practice of medicine, though that, too, would take time since he needed to gain more experience and would have to work in a hospital for that purpose. The thought of exchanging his microscope and zoological charts and exhibits for a stethoscope and vials of pills was so distressing that he felt locked in indecision.

Freud decided to ask Professor Brücke's advice. Perhaps Brücke could offer him some encouragement in the matter of swifter advancement at the Institute, though Fleischl and Exner were ahead of him in priority.

Brücke, with his practical and orderly mind, shook his head reluctantly. There was nothing to do but to go into medical practice. "But this does not have to mean the end of research or growth in knowledge," he encouraged. "Practical success and devotion to truth can be combined if one has the strength and will, as I believe you have."

It was, of course, the only answer Brücke could give, Freud realized, as he left with a heavy heart. He himself had postponed the decision which he had known, in a corner of his mind, had been inescapable from the time he had received his medical degree. Passing the laboratories where he had spent happy hours Freud saw Fleischl-Marxow supervising the efforts of new students. Fleischl turned a pain-drawn face toward him. Freud had not told Fleischl of his courtship of Martha because of the other's own unhappiness in his romantic life. Fleischl had been engaged to a girl for ten or twelve years and now, for some reason, the engagement had been sundered. Perhaps it was Fleischl himself who had broken it, Freud thought, enveloped with pity for the handsome assistant who was now beginning to rely on morphine to relieve the pain of his scarred hand.

He waved and went on swiftly, bidding a silent farewell to all he saw. Although the building was dismal and old it had been his professional home for six years and it was not easy to turn his back on it.

On a Saturday, June 17, 1882, Freud and Martha became secretly engaged. The secrecy was largely because of Martha's mother who did not consider Freud the most promising of suitors. Frau Bernays was very strict in her observance of all orthodox Hebrew rituals and fasts, and Freud's indifference and even hostility to these made him seem a heathen in her eyes. Nor was he financially reliable. Partly to break up the romance, and partly because she constantly yearned to return to Hamburg, the family's former home, Frau Bernays arranged to go there for a month, taking Martha and Minna with her. So the first problem the newly engaged couple had to face was separation and the difficulty of writing to each other without Frau Bernays' knowing.

At Martha's suggestion it was arranged that Fritz Wahle, whom she called an old friend, should act as intermediary. Since Fritz was engaged to someone else, his letters to her from Vienna would not be suspect; he could address the envelopes, with his own name on the return, enclosing missives from Freud. As for her letters, they could reach him at Brücke's Institute in care of the laboratory assistant there.

The mention of Wahle, whom Freud already suspected of being too fond of Martha in spite of his engagement to someone else, made Freud stiffen with jealousy. He fought the emotion down enough to assent to the arrangement. In order to communicate with Martha he would send his letters via the devil if he had to.

Nevertheless, his jealousy continued to fester and, apparently, it was not completely groundless. Fritz did appear to be overly attached to Martha, even to the point where, when matters reached a climax, he threatened to shoot Freud if the latter did not make Martha happy. And lurking right in Hamburg was the distrusted cousin, Max Mayer, who had been of interest to Martha before she was won over by Freud. Overwrought as he was, none of this contributed to Freud's peace of mind and once Martha had departed for Wandsbeck, a suburb of Hamburg, he wrote feverish letters demanding reassurance, or letters accusing her of not truly loving him—letters which he usually followed swiftly with ones of remorse or self-reproach.

Martha Bernays had not chosen an "easy" man for a fiancé. Once he got an idea into his head it was almost impossible to get it out again, no matter how often she said, "Nonsense!" Yet no one could be more gentle or devoted. She had given him a picture of herself before leaving Vienna, concealed in a small elegant box to keep it from prying eyes. The day of her departure, only two days after their secret engagement, he had written to her, "I would so much like to give the picture a place among my household gods that hang above my desk, but while I can display the severe faces of the men I revere, the delicate face of the girl I have to hide and lock away . . . I hardly dare confess how often during the past twenty-four hours I have locked my door and taken it out to refresh my memory."

A month after their engagement day, July 17, Freud appeared in Wandsbeck, unknown to any of Martha's family, and the two arranged a secret rendezvous. There were other secret meetings, and Freud returned home so reassured by Martha's expressions of love and fidelity that he wrote that he was refreshed for a hundred years.

It was a short hundred years. Inwardly, he was convinced that Martha could not truly love him. An artist, as Fritz was, must be much more appealing. Soon Freud was the victim of his own emotions again. These were augmented by his anxiety over his future and by the numerous physical ailments that so often afflicted him, recurring headaches and persistent catarrh among them. Then in late July he was stricken by an anginal swelling which required an incision in his throat. On his little finger was a ring which Martha had given him on the day of their engagement, one which had belonged to her father; he had had a smaller duplicate made for her. In reaction to the pain of the surgeon's thrust Freud banged his hand against the table and broke the ring. For an instant he took this as a bad omen. He dismissed superstition or the thought that perhaps at that moment Martha was tearing his image from her heart, but it took a little struggle for him to do so. For all his dedication to fact and science, irrational and over-imaginative elements in his nature still fought for a place.

On July 31, 1882 Freud began his internship at the General Hospital of Vienna, choosing to begin his studies in surgery. In between his hospital duties he took time to continue some laboratory researches and to write letter after letter to Martha, pouring out his adoration of his "sweet girl" and his hopes for the future. And often he went to stare into the waters of the Danube, watching his reflection ripple and blur on its surface. His love for Martha had revealed depths and emotions in himself he had never suspected before. Why did he, or others, act as they did?

The river gave no answer and he could find none in himself, only dark hints and secrets which left him feeling more confused. He turned with some relief to the discipline of his hospital chores and studies, exhausting though they were.

Fortunately, he thought, he had never needed a great deal of sleep. That, at least, was in his favor, no matter how many other weaknesses he had.

Humbly he had written to Martha, "Can't I too for once have something better than I deserve?" meaning her. But in a later letter he had declared, saying that no matter how much her family loved her, "I will not leave you to anyone . . . no one else's love compares with mine." If necessary, she must forsake Eli, Minna and even her mother for his sake.

Martha was to return in September. In between was the "beastly" month of August during which he must wait, studying anatomical charts, tracing diagrams of arteries and veins into his notebook. All this in order to make a decent living eventually and have Martha safely in a house of their own.

"What is our dowry?" he wrote. "Nothing but love for each other. Nothing else? Now it occurs to me that we would need two or three little rooms to live and eat in and to receive a guest, and a stove in which the fire for our meals never goes out. And just think of all the things that have to go into the rooms! Tables and chairs, beds, mirrors, a clock to remind the happy couple of the passage of time, an armchair for an hour's pleasant daydreaming, carpets to help the housewife keep the floors clean, linen tied with pretty ribbons in the cupboards and dresses of the latest fashion and hats with artificial flowers . . . and an enormous bunch of keys, which must make a rattling noise."

His pen scratched in the silence of his cabinet and he paused, glancing at the familiar room crowded with books, papers and a few pieces of primitive statuary he had extravagantly purchased. It was a very different place from what he had just put on paper for Martha. As soon as possible he must apply for a post at the hospital that would pay at least a nominal salary, and escape the tiresome surgery wards.

He ended his long letter, " . . . without you I would let my arms droop for sheer lack of desire to live; with you, for you, I will make use of them to gain our share in this world so as to enjoy it with you."

CHAPTER 5

Freud and Martha's reunion on her return from Wandsbeck was a happy one, although it had its stormy aspects due largely to Freud's over-possessiveness. She was too subservient to her mother and to her brother Eli, Freud insisted. Freud had always liked Eli, but now his feelings took a different turn. Eli had taken the sixteen-year-old Alex under his wing to teach him something of the practical details of the transportation industry, which was to become Alex's future sphere of work. As was customary for an apprentice, Alex was not entitled to payment. After nine weeks Freud instructed his younger brother to demand payment. Alex, obedient to Freud, did as he was told.

The result was bad feelings on everyone's part and though Martha, torn between conflicting loyalties, finally persuaded Freud to unbend a little, the peace was an uneasy one. He was not a good compromiser and he felt he was right, but not only were he and Martha engaged—Eli was courting Anna with serious intent. It would hardly do to have the Freuds and the Bernays at each others' throats.

In October Freud took a step toward trying to improve his professional and financial status. He called on the great physician, Dr. Hermann Nothnagel, who had just come from Germany to Vienna to occupy the Chair of Medicine at the University. Freud took with him a letter of recommendation from Dr. Theodor Meynert, brain anatomist and director of the Psychiatric Clinic. As a medical student Freud had attended Meynert's lectures on psychiatry and found them stimulating. What Freud hoped, from his interview with Nothnagel, was that the distinguished German would consider him for one of the two assistantships which he had to offer in his department.

He called at Nothnagel's house and presented his letter of introduction from Meynert. Although Nothnagel read it with interest and then asked to see Freud's published scientific articles, he was not encouraging. One of the two assistantships had already been promised, he said, and he could not commit himself in regard to the other.

In that case, Freud asked, could he serve Nothnagel as an Aspirant? The term was not familiar to the German doctor, so Freud explained that in Vienna hospitals the head doctor of a department, called a Primarius, was assisted by a Sekundarius, and the latter was usually promoted from the ranks of the Aspirants. Might he, perhaps, serve as an Aspirant under Nothnagel while waiting for his promotion?

Nothnagel agreed to consider this and Freud left with high hopes. On October 12, thanks partly to Dr. Meynert's speaking in Freud's behalf, Freud was given the job of Aspirant in Nothnagel's Division of Internal Medicine. Stern taskmaster though Nothnagel was, warning his students that anyone who needed more than five hours of sleep a night should not study medicine, Freud was unperturbed. All he needed was four. With the position went a small salary. Freud felt suddenly rich and hastened to tell Martha the good news. Perhaps now he and Martha could plan marriage sooner. First, though, there should be a formal announcement of their betrothal and enough money in his pocket to buy her a regular engagement ring.

On December 26, Freud and Martha made their announcement, Martha wearing a new ring, a plain one with a garnet, on her finger. Frau Bernays gave the pair a reluctant blessing, but Minna, who was sometimes as critical of her mother's demanding ways as Freud was, was delighted. So was her fiancé Ignaz Schönberg.

In January, 1883, Eli and Anna announced their engagement too. Of the three couples, only Eli and Anna could look forward to marriage within the year.

For Freud the months stretched ahead with the promise of more and harder work until such time as he was prepared to start in private practice which could as easily bring failure as success.

He had been thinking vaguely of specializing in dermatology, but though it might be interesting in itself, he could not feel greatly excited about it. Repeatedly, of late, he found himself thinking about something which did excite his imagination, a case of hysteria which his friend and mentor Josef Breuer had worked on from December, 1880 to June, 1882.

Strangely enough, the young woman patient, Bertha Pappenheim, was a onetime friend of Martha's. Twenty-one years old, she had come to Breuer with a confusing number of physical symptoms which seemed to have some connection with her grief over the death of her father since the symptoms appeared after that event. Among the symptoms were a paralysis of her limbs, an inability to see or speak normally, inability to eat with ease and an exhausting, nervous cough. These afflicted her more at some times than at others, depending on her mental state. The young woman was highly intelligent, Breuer had told Freud, but her personality seemed to be split in half. At one moment she would seem like any other normally adjusted person, at others she behaved like a spoiled, naughty little girl. Between the times when she changed personality she seemed to hypnotize herself to sleep and wake up clear-headed. During these clear-headed periods Breuer made it a point to call on her and encourage her to talk about anything and everything, especially the things that seemed most disagreeable in her experience or memory. Among other things, she had frightening hallucinations, daytime nightmares. When she described these to Breuer the terror evaporated.

Because of the relief she felt, she needed little encouragement from Breuer to use the "talking method" more and more. It was she, rather than the doctor, who discovered the value of letting her thoughts and memories flow out in words. In her trance-like states she could sometimes recall how a certain symptom had appeared. If she talked about it and especially its origin, she talked the trouble away. The talking acted as a kind of catharsis, or purging, and was the beginning of what Breuer was to call the "cathartic method."

In order to induce the trance-like states which revealed so much about the young woman's hidden emotions and memories, Breuer began visiting her every morning and putting her under artificial hypnosis, a state superficially resembling sleep and generally brought about by the monotonous repetition of words and gestures while the subject is relaxed.

Breuer had become so engrossed in the case that he could scarcely talk of anything else. He had admitted ruefully to Freud that he had talked so much about it to his wife Mathilde that she had become bored and then jealous, and eventually so unhappy that he decided to bring his patient's treatment to an end and take Mathilde on a trip. The patient was much improved and seemed to accept Breuer's good-by to her calmly; but that evening he was called back and found her in an hysterical state. She twined her arms about Breuer's neck. Further, she imagined that she was pregnant and was actually having imaginary labor pains. Breuer, shocked, calmed her by hypnosis and fled.

The "talking cure," Freud reflected, had not truly cured Breuer's patient permanently, since periods of great improvement had been followed by relapses, but it pointed the way toward a possible technique in ferreting out the hidden motivations of human behavior. Perhaps more important, it indicated that hypnosis, generally derided, could be a valuable medical tool. Hysteria, of course, was nothing new. It could take many forms: wild shouting or crying or childlike tantrums. Sometimes it took the form of blindness, in a person with normal vision, or deafness, though the patient might have perfectly adequate hearing faculties.

Breuer and Freud talked over and over the details of the case Breuer had treated but in spite of how Freud's interest and curiosity were stimulated, his job for the present was to go on through the routine training that would qualify him for a physician's practice.

Freud served under Nothnagel for six months and then transferred to Meynert's Psychiatric Clinic, where he was appointed Sekundararzt. At the same time, May, 1883, he took up lodging in the hospital. He served in Meynert's Clinic for five months, in both the male and female wards, and this constituted his main psychiatric training. Meynert was distinguished in his field and Freud considered him a brilliant genius although he believed that the plump doctor was a better brain anatomist than a psychiatrist.

Although his studies were stimulating, there were times when the corridors in the General Hospital seemed endless to Freud, with their gloomy passages only occasionally illumined by trembling gas lamps, the wards chill in winter in spite of coal stoves burning, and sticky with heat in summer. The sight of hundreds of charity patients, many outcast, and many doomed to painful deaths, did nothing to relieve the generally depressing picture.

Much harder to bear, however, was that Frau Bernays, in June, once again dragged Martha and Minna back to Hamburg, this time for an unstated period. Eli had supported the move, thus increasing Freud's resentment against his onetime friend. Schönberg, too, was up in arms over what he considered Frau Bernays' tyranny. Martha and Minna, who was still waiting for the day when she and Schönberg could marry, were in between the battle lines.

Martha had not fought the move hard enough, Freud insisted in his letters to her. Martha wrote back that she loved him but that she simply could not join him in assaulting her whole family. Bitterly, he wrote, "If you are not what I took you for it is my fault for wooing you without knowing you." Martha fought back in her own way, with reason and patience, until in July, Freud surrendered, promising that she would never hear another harsh word. " . . . I shall lose my loved one if I continue. I have asked of you what is not in your nature, and I have offered you nothing in return . . . you remain for me a precious sweet loved one."

This was perhaps the most difficult period the two went through. It was doubly hard for Freud because of his poverty which prevented him even from buying some modest present for Martha, as he longed to do. His family burdens remained large and he still had not reached the point where his work could lead him to hope of an earlier marriage or professional distinction. In the meanwhile, he was deprived of the presence of the one person whose sympathy meant most to him. The only compensation was that he could indulge himself in long letters directly to Martha instead of writing a "secret record" of devotion, as both she and he had done while she was in Wandsbeck.

Not all of his letters were filled with matters of romance or lovers' quarrels. There were details about his work, even to minute descriptions of an improved way he had found of chemically treating a brain specimen in order to reveal all its cells and fibers. And he confessed that reading certain books was still more interesting than brain anatomy. He had finally obtained a copy of one of his most loved books, *Don Quixote*. Martha, he insisted, must read it too, in spite of parts that might shock her. He also fretted over Martha's health without any apparent cause beyond the paleness of her cheeks and his fear that the amount of kosher food Frau Bernays insisted on was not adequate to a proper diet. Because of his medical involvements and his own poor health, physical well-being was a subject often on his mind. Feeling well was a "precious enjoyment" which he valued for its rarity in his own life.

However, to picture Freud as continually suffering from physical ailments or the general state of anxiety which he called his "neurasthenia" would be a distortion. On the other side was his appreciation of the humor and gaiety of life and his own ability to add to it by a witty phrase or dry observation. He had a talent for winning friends and, underneath his faith in himself and his high ambitions, there was a basic humility. At the same time he was fearless in defending whatever he felt was right or true, and his driving passion was to know what was true.

He tried to learn all he could from the human misery surrounding him in the hospital. On the first of January, 1884, he entered into a department devoted to nervous diseases. This was one of the dreariest departments, in its physical aspects. The wards were so seldom swept that when a broom was used clouds of choking dust flew up. There was no gas light, so that after dusk the patients had to lie in darkness. Freud, like the other doctors, made his rounds by the light of a lantern.

Nevertheless, he was slowly learning to be a doctor. By July his salary had increased. Then he was able to enjoy a short holiday in Wandsbeck with Martha, although he was still not earning enough to marry. He returned, newly determined to make a name for himself in either clinical or pathological medicine.

In the early part of 1884 he had begun to read about the mysterious properties of cocaine, a narcotic drug obtained from coca leaves which helped its users to endure pain and to experience increased energy. He decided to experiment with it in heart disease and nervous exhaustion. Also, he had in mind the case of his friend Fleischl-Marxow. Fleischl was addicted to morphine by now because of the pain in his cancerous hand. Whenever he tried to break the morphine habit his suffering was intense.

As soon as Freud was convinced that cocaine would relieve

pain with no injurious side effects he offered it to Fleischl, who felt there was no way out for himself except suicide. Freud had experimented with the drug on himself and was satisfied that he felt no physical craving for it. In his enthusiasm he even sent some cocaine to Martha to put "fresh roses" in her cheeks. To him it seemed a magical and harmless drug.

Breuer, more cautious, was not impressed. Another colleague was. He was Carl Koller, an intern interested exclusively in eye diseases, especially in the search for a drug that would anesthetize the eye when surgery was needed. One day when Freud was standing in the hospital courtyard with Koller and several other colleagues, one of the interns complained of pain localized in a certain spot in his body. Freud, saying that he had a perfect remedy, went and got a container of cocaine and applied a few drops to the affected area. The intern's pain subsided as Freud had predicted.

As Freud turned away he saw Koller's intense interest. He did not think about the incident until much later when Koller had successfully applied cocaine as a local anesthetic in eye surgery. Freud, due to other distractions, including another visit to Wandsbeck, had missed his own chance for fame in this area.

He continued to recommend cocaine as a kind of universal cure-all, and he was encouraged by Fleischl's first response to the drug. Then, to Freud's consternation, Fleischl began to grow worse. Freud found himself sitting up with his tortured friend night after night. On one of those nights, months after

Fleischl had started taking cocaine, Freud discovered him in such a delirious state that he called Breuer to come and maintain the vigil with him.

Serious cases of cocaine addiction began to be reported in scientific journals. Ultimately, Freud found that instead of his having won the distinction and satisfaction of finding a new way to help and heal mankind, he was being pointed at as a man who had unleashed evil and more suffering, a person of reckless judgment. He had studied and searched with all his mind to try to evaluate cocaine's proper uses, and had insisted, rightly, that addiction was the result of some peculiarity in the patient. For Fleischl, obviously, cocaine had been disastrous, though, as it turned out, he would manage to survive for another six years. Freud suffered humiliation for his mistakes in regard to the drug, but he suffered most because of the consequences to a friend whom he revered.

The path toward greatness was not easy; nor was the path toward financial stability. For all that he tried to save and earn outside money to supplement his hospital allowance, his budget was never balanced, and he had to borrow regularly from Breuer, Fleischl or other friends with means.

He managed somehow to indulge his hunger for buying books and sent copies to Martha and Minna, whose intellectual qualities he admired the more he knew her. He also attended the theatre when he could afford it. A play which made a deep impression on him was Sophocles' tragedy, *Oedipus Rex*, in which, by a series of coincidences and errors, the hero Oedipus killed his father and married his own mother. The play haunted him with the tantalizing thought that under the mythology lay a deeply buried truth which might help to explain some of the hostilities and resentments he had felt toward his own father, as if his father were a rival for Freud's place in Amalie Freud's affections. Yet, on the surface, this seemed incredible. He respected and loved the "old man," as he thought of his father at times, in spite of his weaknesses or failures.

On January 21, 1885, Freud wrote to Martha to tell her that he had applied for the position of Privatdocent; though it paid no salary it would permit him to hold some outside classes and would provide him with prestige invaluable to private medical practice.

In June Freud passed the oral examinations required as the first step in certifying him for the position he coveted. In the same month he won a postgraduate traveling grant which meant he could take a six months' leave from the hospital and receive the grand sum, to him, of six hundred gulden, or about $240.

The night before he received the grant he had a vivid dream. Although there were only two other applicants for the scholarship, Freud dreamed that Brücke, his sponsor, came to him and told him that there were not two but seven other candidates. Before the dream Freud had felt pessimistic about his chance of winning. He woke reassured. He had seven brothers and sisters (including the dead Julius) competing with him for the favored place in the family but had he not always been the winner and favorite?

Once he had won the grant there was no doubt in his mind as to where he would go. To Martha first, and then on to Paris to study with the great French neurologist, Jean M. Charcot.

He wrote exuberantly to his "little Princess": "I am coming with money and staying a long time . . . and then on to Paris to become a great scholar and then come back to Vienna with a huge, enormous halo, and then we will soon get married . . ."

To make his happiness complete, Freud was finally approved as a Privatdocent in Neuropathology. On the last day of August, 1885, he left the General Hospital for good. He had lived and labored there for a little over three years. He was twenty-nine years old.

Sitting in the train clacking on its way toward Hamburg, he contemplated the future. He had made mistakes, he had blundered and he had narrowly missed important discoveries which were within his reach. Nevertheless he felt in his bones that he had some talent that would win him distinction. Perhaps Charcot who was making startling discoveries about hysteria through hypnotism would give him fresh insights into the causes of mental suffering and nervous disorders.

One shadow hovered over his thoughts, the tragedy of Ignaz Schönberg. His lungs were now riddled with tuberculosis and he could not hope to survive. Consequently he had broken his engagement to Minna. Although Freud understood why Schönberg had done this, he thought that even if he were similarly doomed he could never bear to set Martha free.

Freud arrived in Wandsbeck on September 2, and he and Martha spent almost a month together. Martha had promised that she would set a day for their wedding and they discussed this as they walked through gardens or sat on the sofa at the Bernays' house trying to avoid the watchful eyes of Martha's mother, even though the eyes were not as critical or reproachful now as they had been.

One thing Freud insisted upon was that he did not want to go through what he considered the complicated absurdities of a Jewish ceremony, as Eli and Anna had. Not that he had suffered from it; he had refused to go at all, being on non-speaking terms with Eli at the time. Partly Freud had disliked the ceremonies because they required full dress, which he considered a pompous waste.

Martha agreed to Freud's desire for a civil ceremony. It was hard not to agree with someone so full of plans and energy and hope. Besides the grant he had received, a wealthy colleague of his, Josef Paneth, had contributed money toward the Paris trip to see Charcot. And, Freud bragged, he had actually managed to save a few gulden from the time he had spent working in a private sanatorium for people with nervous disorders.

"And I have saved 1800 gulden from the legacy my aunt left me," Martha announced proudly, as they sat discussing their plans in a quiet corner of the house. "Plus what Eli has in trust for me."

Freud figured their riches in the palm of his hand, pretending his forefinger was a pencil, happily trying to estimate what the cost of their honeymoon would be and balancing against that the amount he had promised his family per year for their urgent needs.

Martha looked at him from the corner of her eye, mentally calculating the cost of her trousseau and all the house linen which a bride was expected to bring with her, even as she studied Freud's thoughtful profile. When she had first met Freud's mother she had thought Amalie was fatuous in her admiration for her son.

She didn't exaggerate at all, Martha thought now. Not only was Sigmund handsome with his thick black hair and glossy, neatly trimmed beard, but there was something in his eyes that had exceptional power. Dark, intense, luminous, they sometimes made Martha feel that he could look right through her and through others.

She leaned against him and his arm encircled her waist. A wreath of smoke hung in the air over their heads, a blue reminder of the cigar he had recently extinguished. Her Sigmund, Martha thought happily as he kissed her, had only one fault; he smoked too much.

CHAPTER 6

It was raining and the streets of Paris were so dirty that Freud thought the Roman name for the city, Lutetia, meaning "the muddy town," was an apt one. He had been in Paris less than a week and his disappointment in it was intense. Never had he felt so lonely. The chief things in Paris for which he felt appreciation were those of historical significance, the obelisk from Luxor in the Place de la Concorde, scribbled over with markings dating back a thousand years, and the antiquities wing of the Louvre.

The morning's call at the Charity Hospital of Salpêtrière, where Jean Charcot held sway, had not helped, for Freud had absent-mindedly left his letter of introduction to the famous neurologist at his hotel. Furthermore, Charcot was busy in the wards. He walked on through the rain, hoping his new silk hat and gloves would not be ruined. At a cafe he turned in. One thing Paris did have was delicious coffee. While he sipped it he would take the opportunity to try to improve his halting French by some direct conversation with the waitress and thus gain a little profit from the dreary day.

The next day, October 20, Freud was admitted to Charcot's laboratory in the gloomy, medieval buildings which made up the Salpêtrière. With other silk-hatted guest doctors he sat down to wait for the arrival of Charcot. In an adjoining room was the out-patient clinic where men, women and sometimes children also waited. Some of them exhibited tics, tremors, or signs of paralysis with which Freud had become familiar at the Vienna hospital. Charcot, in volumes of diagnostic studies on such patients, had first traced the symptoms back to physical origins: brain injuries, crippled limbs, various diseases. Eventually, however, Charcot had discovered that not all such symptoms had a physical base, or if they did, laboratory investigations could not reveal what the bases were.

Other doctors said that the illnesses must be imaginary then, if no physical base could be found, but Charcot continued searching for other causes.

As he waited for Charcot to appear Freud thought over his own investigations in this field. Although he believed that there was usually a physical cause for such afflictions as those displayed by the patients in the waiting room, there were so many gaps in the theories about it that he had written monographs of his own challenging the arguments of others. When the monographs were published a few critics said they showed that a penetrating, original mind was at work, but he had received little recognition, and less money.

66

There was a stir in the consultation room. Doctors, interns and assistants looked toward the door. Freud had his first glimpse of the famous Charcot. He was a tall man, nearly sixty years old, clean-shaven, long wisps of hair stuck behind his ears and full protruding lips. With a nod to his colleagues and guests he removed his top hat and immediately began to examine patients, diagnosing their cases aloud.

For the benefit of his professional visitors Charcot set out to prove his theory that hysterical patients, under hypnosis, could be made to produce any symptom suggested to them. By means of hypnotic procedures he placed various patients in a trance, and made each exhibit the symptoms he suggested to them. A woman with perfectly healthy vision became blind when he told her that she could not see, until he ended her hypnosis. A man with strong legs collapsed when Charcot told him that he was crippled. Or, with patients already afflicted with "imaginary" maladies, the opposite effect could be obtained. Under hypnosis the individual who believed he could not lift his arm would raise it easily at a command from Charcot.

The manner in which Charcot demonstrated and lectured struck Freud as masterful. No wonder students from all over the world considered it a passport to success if they were chosen to study with him. At the end of the diagnostic period Freud presented his card with a not altogether steady hand. Yes, he thought, mental anxiety could easily translate itself into a physical symptom.

Charcot fingered the card a moment, then without further

ado invited Freud to accompany him on his rounds. Delighted, Freud stammered his appreciation in French. He felt extra gratitude and a refreshing intimacy when Charcot took the trouble to correct a word which Freud had mispronounced. Charcot then led him through the laboratory, showing him everything of interest, and on to the lecture hall. From there they proceeded to several wards. Without any pompousness Charcot explained many things to Freud and Freud began to feel very much at his ease, even though he considered Charcot one of the greatest of physicians. At the end of the tour his brain felt sated with Charcot's ideas, while many of his own former conceptions lay in ruins.

After this first meeting with Charcot, Freud was given every opportunity to study brain specimens, nerves and nervous disorders at the hospital. But for a long time he had little further personal contact with Charcot. Frustrated, he decided to write Charcot a letter offering his services in translating one of Charcot's books into German. The offer was accepted and the two men became friends; Freud was a guest at the Charcot home several times.

Before long, Freud was writing to Martha that Paris was a city of magic. Charcot was entirely engrossing. The actress Sarah Bernhardt was as remarkable as claimed. As for formal dinner parties requiring swallow tail coats and white ties, they were utterly boring. He had discovered one thing that he and Charcot had in common, though, at one such party at the Charcots' house. Neither could knot a formal white tie properly. Freud, in despair, had worn a ready-made black cravat which Martha had sent him. Charcot had worn a similar one, admitting an inability to tie the white even with his wife's help.

All that he was seeing and experiencing Freud poured out in his letters to his fiancée, including appraisals of himself. "Do you really find my appearance so attractive?" he wrote. "Well, this I very much doubt. I believe people see something alien in me and the real reason for this is that in my youth I was never young and now that I am entering the age of maturity I cannot mature properly . . . Now for a long time I have known that I am not a genius and cannot understand how I ever could have wanted to be one. I am not even very gifted."

At the end of February, 1886, Freud left Paris. Toward the end of his stay, he had felt that his continuing researches via the microscope and brain anatomy were increasingly unrewarding; psychopathology, the study of mental disorders from a psychological point of view, drew him now. Charcot had opened the door a little way; beyond was all new territory.

On his way home Freud spent a few weeks in Berlin in order to study the general disease of children, for he had been offered a post as director of a new neurological department being opened in the first public Institute for Children's Diseases in Vienna. In between his studies, he managed to find time for a trip to Wandsbeck.

Ignaz Schönberg had died shortly after the first of the year, and Martha and Freud tried to subdue their joy at being together again and making definite plans for a fall wedding because of Minna.

Arriving back in Vienna, Freud opened his own private offices as a practicing neuropathologist on April 25, renting a two-room flat for that purpose. The flat was well furnished so that all he had to buy was a couch for patients. Books, bookcases and desk he had. A glass plaque with his name in gold letters decorated the door on the street side, and a porcelain name plate hung on his own door. Both were supplied by Mathilde Breuer in honor of the occasion.

Freud's first consultation fee went to Wandsbeck to buy a feather for Martha, plus some wine for her, Minna and their mother to celebrate the beginning of his private practice.

Besides seeing his own patients, most of whom were sent to him by Breuer, Freud worked regularly at the Kassowitz Clinic for children. He pursued his anatomical researches in Dr. Meynert's laboratory in spite of his now dominant interest in a clinical treatment of mental disorder, continued his translation of Charcot's work and gave two lectures on hypnotism. To add to his work load he was called up for active military service in August and had to spend a month as senior army surgeon in a small town in Moravia.

In spite of his worry about making money and his lack of confidence in his medical abilities, he more than managed to pay for his expenses which he figured at ten gulden ($4.00) a day. Still it was not enough for marriage and raising a family.

Relatives of Martha's saved the day by providing a gift of

money to make the wedding possible, and on September 13, 1886, Sigmund Freud and Martha Bernays were married in a civil ceremony in the Town Hall of Wandsbeck, Germany. They had to be married again, in a Jewish ceremony, however, because Austria, where they were to reside, did not recognize civil marriages.

Martha was then twenty-five years old, Freud thirty. After a month's honeymoon, traveling around Germany, the pair settled down in a four room flat in Vienna, large enough to provide consulting rooms for the doctor of neurology. The first months of marriage were happy ones in spite of Freud's joking prediction that it would be the beginning of a thirty-year war between them.

Actually he felt that the conflicts and quarrels were safely behind them. Most of them had been caused by his own tempestuous nature, he realized. Now that Martha was safely his, the source of his jealousies and romantic frustrations had been removed. Still that did not mean that all was tranquil within himself. Strange anxieties, including the one over train travel, remained, together with other moods or emotions which he could not understand. If one learned to know himself, could he better understand other persons? For the time being he could only continue to watch, listen and experiment, using the tools at hand until better ones could be found. Increasingly he wanted to know why human beings acted as they did.

The two lectures Freud had given on the possible use of hypnosis in medical treatment had caused some raised eyebrows among his Vienna colleagues. A few were openly antagonistic. One of his foes, he began to feel, was his former advisor and friend, Professor Meynert. It had not helped their relationship that Freud had pointed out errors in Meynert's researches on the brain.

On October 15, Freud delivered a lecture at the Society of Physicians' meeting, a report on what he had learned from Charcot. The lecture was called "On Male Hysteria," and in it Freud advanced Charcot's theory that hysteria in men was no different from hysteria in women, that both showed the same symptoms. Before Charcot's studies, hysteria was generally believed to be "imagination" and an ailment which was almost exclusively confined to women. The very word "hysteria," the doctors of the time emphasized, came from the Greek word hystera, meaning womb, and the malady had long been called "mother-sickness." Although cases of male hysteria had been known, most physicians blamed a physical cause such as an accident, or diseases, like epilepsy. Now Freud was emphasizing the role of psychology, an emphasis that was especially unwelcome to neurologists or brain specialists who had built their practice on treating hysteria as a bodily malfunction.

As Freud spoke he felt the increasing coldness of the majority of the audience. Coldest of all was Theodor Meynert. At last, Meynert stood up and said, his voice edged with sarcasm:

"Perhaps Doctor Freud will prove his point to us by producing a case of male hysteria with the kind of symptoms he has described."

Freud replied as calmly as he could that he had seen such cases in Paris. Charcot, in fact, had set aside a special ward for hundreds of men so afflicted. Meynert and most of the other doctors continued to look at him with cynicism or hostility. Bitterness filled Freud. Did these men want to investigate facts or did they only want to cling to their comfortable beliefs? Meynert had challenged him openly; he must meet the challenge.

"I will gladly produce such a case," Freud declared, looking at Meynert.

This turned out to be unexpectedly difficult. There were several cases of male hysteria in the General Hospital but the senior physicians in charge refused to let Freud make use of them for his purpose. They claimed that the men were suffering from actual paralysis, not a hysterical form, or real blindness instead of blindness provoked by hysteria. Arguing with them, Freud realized that there was more than wilful ignorance involved in the opposition of the hospital staff; they were afraid to risk the anger of a powerful person like Meynert.

Once he had started something, Freud would not and could not give up. Before long, with the help of a young laryngologist who was sympathetic, he found a patient outside the dominion of the medical hierarchy. The man was a twenty-nine-year-old laborer who had had a serious quarrel with his brother. The quarrel had affected his emotional and nervous system so violently that his vision was blurred, his color sense awry.

Freud presented his case before the Society of Physicians, November 26. The evidence was conclusive enough for him to receive applause. He went home feeling triumphant. He soon learned that the applause was a superficial gesture and that the opposition to his line of research into psychic disorders was as strong as ever. He was shut out of the laboratory of cerebral anatomy shortly after his "triumphant" lecture. For a whole session of the University he had no place to deliver lectures because of the hostility of the authorities.

To Martha he said bitterly that he might as well turn his back on the University. Henceforward he would devote himself to his own practice, using his patients as his research material.

But in his own practice he met one challenge after another; so many that he wondered if he should claim to be a neurologist at all. The lame, the halt and the blind came to him, not charity cases but members of the elite of Vienna society: women with trembling fits for which there seemed no cause; men with heart spasms which had no discernible physical reason; even children quaking or stuttering with terror though no overt menace could be found.

Over and over Freud heard himself prescribing the same futile, time-worn remedies: take hot baths, journey to a health resort, arrange for relaxing massages, exercise, get more fresh air. Patients would sometimes grow better following such therapy, only to return in worse shape than before. At times Freud was tempted to believe that these persons' mysterious illnesses were imaginary, as some of his colleagues claimed. But the symptoms were not imaginary; the tremors, the paralysis, the numbness to sensation were very real.

Vainly Freud searched through medical manuals looking for some effective method of therapy, and experimented with modern electrical treatments to stimulate the nerves. He thought more often of Breuer's "talking treatment" in the case of the hysterical Bertha Pappenheim—for years he had been urging Breuer to write a paper on the case—and of Breuer's use of hypnosis. Freud made up his mind. No matter how much the majority of physicians scorned hypnosis he would try it out, even though it might mean his professional ruin. The one thing he could not do was to follow the easy and often indifferent attitude of his fellow neurologists in treating their tormented patients, though this was the path to success of a kind and affluence.

Money was certainly needed, especially with his and Martha's first child on the way. If the child turned out to be a girl, he reflected, he would want to call her Mathilde in honor of Josef Breuer's wife.

Mathilde Freud was born October 16, 1887. At 12:30 in the morning the exhausted but exuberant father wrote the news to Martha's mother and Minna, although he had already sent them a telegram.

Of his new daughter, he wrote, "She weighs nearly seven pounds, which is quite respectable, looks terribly ugly, has been sucking her right hand from the first moment . . . and behaves as though she really feels at home here." As for Martha, "She has been so good, so brave and sweet all the way through . . . when she had to scream she apologized each time to the doctor and the midwife."

He sat back, puffing on a cigar, relaxing for the moment in his role of husband, father and family man.

"Goodnight," he ended the letter, "I trust you will soon write again to your little family consisting of Martha, Mathilde and Sigmund."

Beginning in December, Freud turned to hypnosis as a way of trying to bring relief to patients with nervous disorders which had no discoverable physical basis. For a year and a half he experimented intensely with this technique, using the power of suggestion to try to effect a cure while a patient was in a dreamlike trance. Freud had many successes with the technique but he also had defeats. Some patients could not be hypnotized. Others often relapsed into their old symptoms once they left off treatment. Aside from this, Freud had to face his own boredom at repeating hypnotic procedures day after day and asserting, "When you wake, you will have no trembling," or stammer or paralysis.

Even though his experiments with hypnosis did not turn out as he had hoped, he learned much about the individual lives of his patients and some of the secret motivations behind their symptoms. Combining hypnosis with the cathartic method, or talking cure, he found that one reason why patients treated by hypnosis had relapses later was that during treatment they responded as the doctor suggested simply to please him. The success or failure of the hypnotic method depended to a great extent on the personal relationship between doctor and patient. Some women patients entered so deeply into the relationship that, to Freud's chagrin, they showed every sign of having fallen in love with him, as Bertha Pappenheim had during Breuer's medical treatment.

Discussing these matters with Breuer, Freud struggled to find a deeper pattern under nervous or neurotic behavior, one suggesting that the sexual life of many patients had much to do with their actions. Breuer shied away from such a suggestion. One possibility they agreed on, however, and explored in their talks and studies, was that hysterical attacks came about because a memory got stuck somewhere. Normally, they speculated, memories, with their particular energies, were worked off within the nervous system or found an outlet in action. But if memories were too painful they were pushed aside or buried in a deeper level of consciousness beyond the control of reason. Then, if some spark touched them off, they spilled over into the nervous system, bringing an overload of nervous or emotional energy that could only be discharged through a hysterical attack.

Before Freud and Breuer had begun to reach this theory, Freud had devoted much time to a study of aphasia, a condition in which the victim loses the power of speech, or suffers impairment of the ability, or cannot understand the language of others. In 1890, when Freud tackled the problem of aphasia, medical science asserted that brain injuries called "lesions" were responsible, and that all nervous disorders stemmed from such lesions often located in unknown areas of the brain. Nothing, or very little, could be done to help such cases, said Freud's colleagues, including his famous teacher Meynert.

Freud decided that such views were false. An injury to the brain would disturb more than just the power of speech or communication. The brain was not an apartment house which could be neatly divided into rooms, one room controlling the ability to speak, another controlling muscular coordination and yet another the sense of touch or smell. From his studies—and Freud read all the available information—he was forced to conclude that somehow the physiological and the psychic were separate. Otherwise everything could be explained by anatomy, every psychic function traced to a certain part of the brain. Psychology was not that simple he realized, although, steeped in the teachings of his day, he thought it might be possible sometime to trace psychic functions back to a physiological basis. In the meantime he felt that a new approach should be made, in which one should study actual behavior and draw a strict line between physiological and psychological data.

In 1891 Freud published a short book, *On Aphasia*, which is generally considered his most important work on neurology. Also, it contains the seeds of the ideas he was to develop later, ideas which would increasingly influence his practice and his whole approach to the problem of mental disorders. His colleagues were standing still; he was moving swiftly ahead, no matter what the risk. In the same year, 1891, he collaborated with a pediatric assistant at the Kassowitz Children's Institute on an exhaustive monograph dealing with paralyses in children. This, and other papers on related subjects, helped him to become a leading authority on children's paralyses of that time.

In 1892 Freud made his first attempt at treating a patient entirely by what he called "psychical analysis," dispensing with hypnotism entirely. The woman, whom he called Elizabeth von R., had an array of physical symptoms, including leg pains, arising from mental or emotional disturbances which Freud discovered were caused by her unconscious attraction to her brother-in-law.

The method he used with Fraulein Elizabeth was to have her lie down, close her eyes and concentrate on a particular symptom, then try to recall any memories that would throw light on its origin. Whenever she found herself unable to recall anything, or very little, Freud would press her forehead with his hand, insisting that if she kept trying the recollections would come. The method worked with this patient and with others. Besides insisting on the patient's trying to remember past experiences, he encouraged the patient to express everything that came to mind, even though it might seem unpleasant, shocking or irrelevant. In this way "forgotten" memories often came to light, ones which bore a direct relationship to the patient's troubling symptoms.

In the case of Fraulein Elizabeth, Freud accidentally picked up a valuable insight into improving his technique in psychical analysis. Just as the woman was talking fluently he asked a question, thus interrupting the flow of her thoughts. She herself criticized him for this and he realized that she was entirely justified. It was a mistake which he would not repeat.

At times in these years, Freud felt more like a detective than a doctor. Underneath what his patients said and did there lurked things they avoided mentioning, secret guilts and fears. Usually they did not even know their own guilts. It was easier for such persons to develop pains in their legs, or nervous disabilities, and concentrate on those instead of searching their own minds. Painful memories were pushed aside, only to return in physical affliction or states of unreasonable anxiety like the "demons" of the Middle Ages. Freud was seeking a scientific form of exorcism.

CHAPTER 7

Freud's family was growing. His first son, called Martin, though he was named Jean Martin after Charcot, was born December 6, 1889. On February 19, 1891, Oliver, named for one of Freud's early heroes, Oliver Cromwell, arrived. Although Martha ruled the domestic affairs of the household, she appeared to be completely subservient to Freud in the choosing of names for their children, for all were named for persons close to him.

With the increase of the family, more space was needed. According to one story, Freud and Martha spent much time planning what their new home would be like. Then, one day after he was through with his consultations, Freud went for a walk and saw a "For Rent" sign on a house. He investigated and decided that it was exactly the house he must have, although it was gloomy and lacked a number of the features he and Martha had agreed were necessary.

Whatever Martha's reaction, the Freuds moved into the new combined home and office, and Berggasse 19 was their address for the next forty-seven years until Hitler's armies came marching into Austria, sweeping art, science and human lives before them.

Three more children were born at Berggasse 19. Ernst, born in 1892, was the namesake of Ernst Brücke; Sophie, 1893, was named after the daughter of a beloved former teacher of Freud's; and finally Anna, the last child, born 1895, was named after the same teacher's niece.

Freud was a fond and loving father. The laughter of his and Martha's children made him write, " . . . we imagine it is the loveliest thing that can happen to us." When illnesses struck the children, as they commonly did, he was both concerned father and worried doctor.

When Mathilde, five or six years old, contracted diphtheria, Freud was distraught with worry. He and Martha moved the child's bed into their own room and kept a constant vigil, Freud leaving only long enough to take care of his patients in the offices below the living quarters. Josef Breuer, the family physician, did all he could but it seemed that Mathilde would die. Although great strides were being made in an understanding of diphtheria, a disease in which a grayish membrane builds up to clog the victim's throat, most doctors could do little more than try to suck the membrane out through a tube; in dire circumstances, they might open the windpipe with a knife to help the patient breathe.

Leaning over the bed where his oldest child lay in a high

fever, scarcely able to breathe or swallow, Freud asked her desperately what she would most like to have in the world. Whatever it might be, he promised recklessly, he would get it for her. Mathilde managed to say, "A strawberry."

It was September and strawberries were out of season but Freud set out to try to find some. He hailed a fiakre, a two-horse cab, a vehicle more expensive than the public tram or one-horse cab he normally used in order to stretch his income. He ordered the driver to hurry toward a famous shop which carried all sorts of unusual delicacies. There he found the needed berries and rushed back home.

He leaned over his daughter's bed once again, Martha watching with fear-racked eyes as Freud placed a strawberry on Mathilde's tongue. Mathilde attempted to swallow the fruit. It lodged in her swollen throat and she began to cough violently. For a moment it seemed she must strangle to death when, suddenly, she coughed out the berry. With it came the diseased membrane which had been closing her throat. This marked the beginning of her recovery.

That night when he went to bed Freud wondered if he might not have a nightmare over the events of the day, although he had discovered in his own experience that the chronology of dreams was seldom logical. His especially seemed unruly. As he had once told Martha, he never dreamed about matters which had occupied him during the day. Dreams were very curious things, and they had interested him for many years so that he had not only observed his own but often recorded them. All his life he had been what he called a "good dreamer," meaning that he had many dreams. Some persons he talked to said that they could not remember their dreams at all or, if they could, the dreams were so senseless it didn't matter.

Did any dreams make sense? Freud wondered. If so, what kind of sense? Or what was the difference between dreams in real sleep and the dreamlike state in the "artificial sleep" of hypnosis. Could dreams provide useful clues to the hidden processes of the psyche?

There were more questions in the world than answers, thought Dr. Sigmund Freud as he dealt with an increasing number of patients, or pursued his scientific books, or went vacationing to the mountains with his family in summer to escape Vienna's intense heat. Although his income was still modest, such vacations were almost a physical necessity for the family's health and his own, as were his individual journeys to visit colleagues or only to satisfy his travel lust. Whenever Freud set out for a journey he arrived at the train station an hour or more early, still troubled by an unreasonable anxiety that he would miss the train. He once described his fear as a "phobia." But such a condition of morbid dread usually prevents its victim from doing what he wishes to do, and Freud's dread never prevented him from going where he wanted to go.

Breuer, watching Freud in those days when Freud's searching intellect was scouring every cranny of consciousness and human motivation in an attempt to understand, said that he felt like a hen watching a hawk soar overhead. Breuer had finally let himself be persuaded by Freud to collaborate on an article on hysteria based on cases they had both studied. The article was published in a scientific journal in January, 1893. The two men were at the same time working on a book to be called *Studies on Hysteria*, based on case histories. Breuer's contribution was the case of Bertha Pappenheim, known in the published book as "The Case of Anna O."

More and more, Freud suggested that behind people's actions, desires, and nervous disturbances, there might be deep, unconscious guilts or confusions having to do with the sexual instinct. So powerful an instinct could not be ignored, Freud contended; in fact, it might well be more powerful than any other as a motivator of human acts. Much as he admired his younger colleague, Breuer drew back. Human beings possessed a bundle of appetites and instincts, as well as their mental and spiritual qualities. It was dangerous and a distortion to emphasize one instinct above the rest.

For Freud there was only one principle on which to base honest inquiry; study the facts and study them again. He realized that he often learned more from his patients than he gave. When they babbled of their dreams, as they so often did, he treated these too as facts to be studied, instead of dismissing them as nonsense like most of the medical world. Looking at his patients day after day, encouraging them to tell him of their most secret longings or fears, he found that under the surface structure of their lives the "basements" contained an astonishing array of guilts and desires which threatened to pull down the whole house. Some indulged in actions or fantasies which seemed too shameful to themselves to reveal to his listening ear, though Freud was never shocked by the forms certain aberrations took any more than a surgeon would be shocked by an inflamed appendix. He saw before him only a suffering human being whom he longed to understand more completely and help. Part of the reason that he could feel sympathy instead of censorship was that he was all too aware of the unresolved conflicts in his own psyche. Although he had never suffered actual paralysis in his body he was sometimes strangely paralyzed in his will to work, and painful moods still seized him. The words that Jesus Christ had spoken in a Nazarene synagogue centuries before were ones he could address to himself: "Physician, heal thyself." He would be his own patient, one on whom he would spare nothing in the way of searching analysis.

From 1887 to 1902, Freud wrote out his thoughts and research experiments to a new friend, Wilhelm Fliess, a physician and biologist in Berlin. Fliess, two years younger than Freud, had come to Vienna in 1887 for postgraduate study and attended some lectures Freud was giving on anatomy and the nervous system. The two felt a mutual attraction and for a couple of years corresponded regularly, addressing each other as "Sigmund" and "Wilhelm." They arranged to meet and talk together for several days at a time in what they called "congresses."

To Fliess, Freud wrote many of his most intimate feelings with detailed descriptions of his researches. "I am pretty well alone here in tackling the neuroses," he told his friend. "They regard me rather as a monomaniac, while I have the distinct feeling that I have touched on one of the great secrets of nature." He was referring to his growing conviction that neuroses were acquired owing to disturbances of sexual life.

In April, 1894, Freud grew worried about the irregularity of his heartbeat and described all his symptoms carefully to Fliess. "It is painful for a medical man, who spends all the hours of the day struggling to gain an understanding of the neuroses, not to know whether he is himself suffering from a reasonable or a hypochondriacal depression." Fliess had strongly urged Freud to give up smoking—he smoked as many as twenty cigars a day, at times—though Fliess, on examining him previously, had said he did not have a "nicotine heart." Now in an over-anxious state, Freud's concern was tinged with hypochondria, an exaggerated fear for his physical condition and an apprehensiveness that he might not have long to live. At both Fliess's and Breuer's advice he cut down on his smoking and managed to limit himself for fourteen months to one cigar a week.

His real tyrant was not smoking, however. He wrote to Fliess in 1895: "My tyrant is psychology; it has always been my distant, beckoning goal . . . During recent weeks I have devoted every free minute to such work; the hours of the night from eleven to two have been occupied with imaginings, transpositions, and guesses, only abandoned when I arrived at some absurdity . . . You must not ask me for results for a long time yet."

Nevertheless, he was moving rapidly ahead. In the same

year, 1895, his and Breuer's *Studies on Hysteria* was published, a book which was a major step forward in the beginning of the method of analysis which Freud was to develop to such an extent that "psychoanalysis" as he finally called it, became a household word. Breuer and Freud held different conclusions from their studies of hysteria, differing on some basic points, but Freud never failed to credit the contribution Breuer made toward the advancement of his own theories.

The book received a good deal of attention from both medical and lay periodicals, most of it critical or indignant. Breuer winced under the criticisms; Freud, though wounded, tried to be philosophical or to laugh off comments that seemed to him to be based on ignorance or rancor. The rebuffs only increased his determination to persevere in the direction he had taken. Eight hundred copies of the *Studies* were printed, but in thirteen years only 626 copies were sold.

Even before the publication of the book, relations between Breuer and Freud had been increasingly strained, both because of their divergence in theory and apparently because of a growing conflict between their personalities. It was no help, in a man as proud and independent-minded as Freud, that he owed Breuer a good deal in money loans. Also, his emotions had still not been greatly softened or brought under control for all his attempts at understanding them, and he was in some ways as temperamental as during his courtship days. He began to complain to Fliess that it was impossible to get along with Breuer any more. Gradually the long friendship came to an end, a pattern that was not new in Freud's life, and would be repeated to some extent in his relationship with Fliess.

The year 1895 was important most of all because it was then that Freud made his first formal and concentrated attempt to analyze one of his own dreams from beginning to end. This happened during the summer when the family was staying at Schloss Bellevue near the mountain called the Kahlenberg. Such vacation trips, as well as the fact that the Freuds employed a governess, a children's nurse, a full-time cook, and a housemaid who also acted as a receptionist to Freud's patients, would make it seem that Freud had become well-to-do. Actually, he was still plagued by debts (including the one to Breuer which his honor demanded he repay though Breuer did not) and had all he could do to keep afloat financially. For members of the middle class of his time, human servants were what mechanical servants—automobiles, automatic washing machines and dryers, and even television sets—are today. They were not considered luxuries but necessities if one wanted to have a smoothly run household as Martha did. Her duties included not only managing and raising a family but seeing to it that nothing interfered with Freud's work. Nothing, in fact, was permitted to, insofar as this was within her power. As for summer sojourns in the mountains, everyone in Vienna who could possibly afford to do so fled from the heat. Freud himself seldom joined his family for the whole period, normally sending them on ahead of him a month earlier while he remained in his office.

Freud had analyzed thousands of his patients' dreams before 1895, but it was when he studiously analyzed one of his own that he felt he had captured the secret key which would turn the lock of understanding. The dissection he made of his dream, and his interpretations of it, was to cover many printed pages in his great and famous book, *The Interpretation of Dreams*. The "secret" was one which he stated simply in his conclusion of the analysis. "When the work of interpretation has been completed, we perceive that a dream is the fulfillment of a wish."

It would be over four years before his studies were completed to his satisfaction, and the book published, but he had found the cornerstone around which his theory of dreams would be built. Dreams, he perceived, were the royal road to the unconscious part of man's existence, and the unconscious was a far larger sphere than the conscious.

Up until this period of his life Freud had worked mainly with the relationship between the body and mind. Neurology, concentrated on the nervous system and its diseases, was a confused and confusing branch of medicine for most practitioners. Neurologists lumped together all patients with curious symptoms as neurasthenics without knowing, themselves, what they meant by the term. If Freud had been willing to accept this way of diagnosing patients, prescribing time-worn but generally useless remedies in the way of electrical treatments, massage, or relaxation, he could probably have settled down to a comfortable practice and gained the respectability that Breuer prized. But he could not; nor could he abandon his growing conviction that sexual disturbance was at the root of neurasthenia or neuroses, nervous disorders without any demonstrable physical lesion.

In May, 1896 Freud gave an address to the Society of Psychiatry and Neurology in Vienna, again advancing his theories on hysteria. The famous German psychiatrist, Krafft-Ebing, who himself had done a comprehensive study on mental disorders, said that Freud's paper sounded "like a scientific fairy tale." After that Freud read only one more paper in Vienna, eight years later.

Back he went to his consulting room and his study at Berggasse 19, to mull over once again the things he had been learning from his patients and from his own probings. He still used hypnotism as a tool, if it seemed helpful, but he relied increasingly on urging the patient to relax and talk freely. In March, 1896, he described his method, which he was slowly perfecting, as "psycho-analysis," for the first time.

One of his main problems in this method was to get his patients to talk freely about their troubles in a way that would bring hidden frustrations, fears or guilts to light where they could be confronted and worked with. Blocks which he called "resistance" to remembering, interfered. It was the doctor's, or psychoanalyst's, job to try to remove these blocks. This, he began to realize, could take months or years in stubborn cases. Few persons could afford the money for such long treatment.

In his preoccupation with his work there were times when he scarcely saw his family except at mealtimes. Minna Bernays was a part of the family now, having moved in to stay and help after the birth of Anna. Mittagessen, the main meal, was served promptly at one o'clock. At the stroke of one everyone in the household would seat themselves at the long dining room table. One door would open to let the maid enter with a tureen of soup, while another door opened to allow Freud to walk from his study to his place at the head of the table. He and Martha faced each other, the children and Minna ranged on each side. If a child was missing Freud would gesture with his fork at the empty chair, silently questioning his wife for the reason.

Freud devoted much of his free time to his mother. His visits to her, usually on a Sunday morning, and her visits in turn to the Berggasse quarters for Sunday afternoon dinner, became a lifelong pattern. Although she sometimes complicated his life by still wanting to control it, if only by advice, he accepted such demonstrations as evidences of her love. Any son who was his mother's favorite, as he was, had a great advantage in life, Freud felt, because of the security it gave him. He was devoted to his mother, also, and their relationship was one of the most important in his life.

His relationship toward his father was more ambiguous, though he felt strong affection and respect for the now old and physically failing man. In some ways, his feeling for his father went deeper than for his mother, deeper, in fact, than he knew.

It was not until his father, aged eighty-one, died in October of 1896, that Freud realized the extent of his ties to Jakob. The death came when Freud was in what he called a "critical period" as far as his own psychic probings went, and he wrote to Fliess that his father's dying left him feeling as if he had been "torn up by the roots. By one of the obscure routes behind the official consciousness the old man's death affected me deeply . . . with his peculiar mixture of deep wisdom and imaginative light-heartedness he meant a great deal in my life. By the time he died his life had long been over, but at a death the whole past stirs within one."

The past, his and everyone else's, was not always truly "past." Long ago events or emotions, though not consciously remembered, maintained their power to affect the present. Some of those forgotten "memories" were at work in him now, acting like a kind of yeast that lifted submerged, past events only part way to the surface of thought.

He must make a far more heroic effort to bring those unconscious memories and stirrings to the surface, he resolved, than he had done so far. But, like his own patients, he held back, an inner resistance operating in him as in them. Was it even possible for one to analyze oneself as deeply as he contemplated? Throughout history, philosophers, religious leaders, artists and writers had pursued and captured glimpses of what went on beneath the surface of man's mind. But what he wanted was something more intense and as daring as a surgeon's taking the scalpel to his own flesh.

CHAPTER 8

The summer following his father's death marked a turning point in Freud's life. He, who in later years would be noted for a deep serenity of spirit, was in 1897 going through what he himself called a kind of neurotic experience which threatened to bring him to a complete breakdown. At times he felt totally unable to work but would wander restlessly from one distraction to another, playing chess or cards or mechanically studying ancient maps. Martha, for all her love and attention to every practical detail that would give him comfort, watched helplessly.

Freud's physical health plagued him also. His old enemy, migraine headache, afflicted him regularly, and he had long been a sufferer from nasal catarrh and sinus trouble. Twice, Fliess operated on him to drain off pus collected in the antrums, hollow spaces in the bone above the nose. Financial pressures, too, remained a problem. Aside from the expenses for his own family he had to contribute to the support of his mother and his two remaining unmarried sisters, Adolfine and Paula. Anna and Eli had emigrated to America. Alexander was doing well in his transportation management work, but though he helped out with the expenses of their sisters and mother he was not rich.

Even in his theoretical work Freud received a stunning blow. For years he had believed what some of his hysterical women patients had told him, that as children they had been sexually seduced by their own fathers or by other close male relatives. He had at first been astonished and disbelieving but then later was convinced that all hysteria was caused by this particular kind of traumatic experience—a severe shock injury to the psyche. Now he realized that these patients had lied, or not lied so much as that they had been deceived by their own memories and confused hysterical fantasies. Underneath, however, there was a reality, the reality of sexual impulses even in childhood. In spite of this insight, which he was to develop further, his pride suffered for the error he had made. It never occurred to him to try to conceal his mistake, however. The only thing to do was to admit that he had been led astray, abandon his theory and go on.

All these pressures, in addition to his strong reaction to his father's death and a beginning of conflict in his friendship with Fliess, worked to make him face the need to begin an intense self-analysis. This he started in July, 1897, combining it with his continuing study of dreams, especially his own dreams.

"I believe I am in a cocoon," he wrote to Fliess, "and God knows what kind of beast will creep out of it."

In attempting to psychoanalyze himself Freud was as much a pioneer as all who set off to travel uncharted paths have been. He had no guide except his own mind and intuition, no resources except his courage and unsparing self-honesty. It was an overwhelmingly lonely form of exploration, this going down into the labyrinth of oneself. During the process he began to experience all the things that as a third party he had witnessed going on in his patients, days when he went about depressed because he had understood nothing of the day's dreams, fantasies or mood. Then there were other days when, like a flash of lightning, understanding would come and the dark corners would be revealed.

The month of July was full of heat, rain and storm. Only the thought of joining his family at a vacation resort at Alt-Aussee on the Alt-Aussersee in Styria helped to sustain Freud's spirits. There the woods would be cool and full of mushrooms and he and the children could go on one of their regular hunts for these, an occupation he enjoyed as much as they.

In August Freud arrived at the cottage Martha had rented. The coolness of the Alps, the beautiful Tyrolean scenery where blue lakes mirrored mountains and pine trees, were like a healing medicine to him, as was the laughter and happy shouts of his children. Anna was still a baby and Sophie four years old. But Mathilde and the boys were more than equal to expeditions in the woods.

Freud knew which were the edible mushrooms and he took great care to show the children which of the many kinds of fungi common to the damp climate at Alt-Aussee were safe to pick and eat. Every mushroom, no matter who found it, was examined by Freud before it was put into the basket to be taken home. He was a swift and tireless walker but he slowed his pace for the youngsters. Dressed in knickerbockers, Norfolk jacket, thick stockings and boots, and wearing a green hat which sported a little chamois brush on one side, he looked the part of a fashionable mountaineer. When he spotted a choice mushroom he would approach it with exaggerated stealth, take off his hat and then suddenly clap it down over the plant, much to the delight of the children. Rarely when the season for picking mushrooms was right did the happy hunters under their paternal captain arrive home without a full basket of the delicacies for their mother and Tante Minna to prepare.

Freud spent six weeks with the family that summer of 1897, staying long enough to be caught in one of the worst floods that the region had known. Bridges were washed away, roads covered with water and shops in Alt-Aussee closed their doors because they had run out of supplies. After three days food at the Freud cottage ran low. Self-analysis was one thing; a diminishing larder with five hungry children was another. On the fourth morning of the flood, Freud came from his room dressed in heavy boots and his mountaineering clothes.

"Where are you going in all this rain, Papa?" Martin asked.

"To try to find a village where there are shops with food to sell." Freud had a look of determination on his face, as if he were going to battle.

That evening a weary but triumphant Herr Doktor Freud came trudging over the landscape, his wet knapsack bulging. The children ran to open the door. With a cheer they watched as he came inside and began pulling a large sausage and crusty loaves of bread from his bag.

The moments of play or adventure with his family were precious to Freud, not only for the relaxation they gave him but for the opportunity they provided to watch the growth and development of his own children. This could be both delightful and instructive. Children, lacking the inhibition of adults, often said or did things which gave him valuable clues to human behavior in general. And in his children's dreams he found many evidences of the wish-fulfillment theory he was developing. Ernst, disappointed in not being able to climb a certain mountain, dreamed that he stood on its summit. Mathilde, much taken by a twelve-year-old boy in a neighbor cottage, dreamed that he moved in with her own family. Martin, excited over reading legends of Greece, dreamed that he was driving in a chariot with Achilles. Little Anna, deprived of food for one day because of a sorely upset stomach, called out in her sleep for strawberries and pudding and everything else that she especially liked to eat.

Back home in Vienna in October, Freud pressed ahead with self-analysis and the study of dreams, his pen busily covering pages of manuscript paper as he recorded theory and experience in the clear, readable style that is typical of all his writings. When not writing he might sit brooding, looking at the large collection of figurines and primitive sculpture that took up more and more space in his study. The year before he had made a trip to Bologna and Ravenna with Alexander and, finally, to Florence. Freud fell in love with Italy, especially the Galileo Museum near Florence with its ancient cultural treasures. Now examples of Florentine statuary were among his treasures. Often while sitting listening to a patient, he would take a figurine or paperweight or other object from his collection and sit turning it over and over in his hands as if the handling of some physical object increased the pitch of his mental concentration. He did the same thing now, while burrowing into his own mind and memories.

He had become convinced that the first years of an individual's life had a profound effect on his personality and character. Experiences entirely forgotten by the conscious part of the mind remained in the unconscious as in a dimly lighted storehouse, affecting action and thought. Only by probing that dimness with a strong searchlight could one hope to see through to the springs of individual behavior. Dream study and psychoanalysis, he believed, were the twin searchlights to reveal the past and thereby perhaps cure psychoneuroses.

One of his own dreams particularly interested him: a dream of a man with one eye, short, fat and high-shouldered, who seemed to be a doctor. Reflecting on the dream later, he had decided the dream figure must represent a one-eyed professor he had once had. However, he had liked the professor, but he had felt a distinct dislike for the one-eyed man in his dream.

On his Sunday call at his mother's he asked her to describe the doctor who had delivered him when he had been born. Amalie readily recalled that the doctor had been one-eyed and, in fact, matched every other characteristic in Freud's dream.

But why the dislike for the dream doctor then? Freud mused. Surely he didn't resent the man's help in bringing him into the world.

"He's the same doctor," his mother added, "who treated you when you fell from a stool and cut open your jaw on the table."

Freud touched the spot where his beard covered the scar. Consciously he remembered nothing of the accident which had happened when he was three, but obviously his unconscious did and had associated the pain of the event with the one-eyed doctor, thus creating the dream feeling of resentment.

Excited, Freud questioned his mother about other childhood matters. He had dreamed that the nurse who cared for him was a thief, which seemed incredible. It was only the truth, his mother told him.

"Of course," she said, "she was an elderly woman. She was always taking you to church. When you came home you used to preach, and tell us all about how God conducted His affairs. All the shiny Kruezers and Zehners and toys that had been given you were found among her things. Your brother

Philipp went himself to fetch the policeman. You were only two and a half then." She pushed some specially made coffee cake toward him. "But why all this going back in time? You're too young to be living in the past—or perhaps you are gathering notes for somebody to do a biography?"

Freud, touched and amused by his mother's unlimited faith in his ultimate fame, smiled ruefully, explaining as simply as he could what his motivations were. Then he changed the subject to praise of her coffee cake.

Amalie sat back, content. He, of whom she saw all too little for her satisfaction, was here; he was devouring her cake with proper appetite; and, most gratifying of all, she had contributed something to the furtherance of his work.

Freud, walking homeward, thought somberly about his energetic mother. She was only twenty-one years older than he. What would happen to her if he should die before she did, her life centered around his as it was? This was an anxiety which nagged him recurrently, even though the fear might have no more foundation than his own mental depression. At the moment, excitement over the causes of certain confusing dreams was uppermost and his thoughts turned to his work.

Hours later, at close to midnight, Freud was busy writing page after page to Wilhelm Fliess. It was true, he admitted, that coincidence might be involved in the way his dreams had matched up with actual childhood incidents but there were other factors which made this unlikely. He went on to describe the complexities and ramifications.

"Being entirely honest with oneself is a good exercise,"

Freud wrote, but intensely difficult. So far he had gained only one new general idea from his self-analysis but it seemed an important one. Part of the idea he owed to the Greek play *Oedipus Rex* which had long fascinated him. In the play Oedipus unwittingly marries his own mother and murders his father.

Was it not possible, Freud conjectured, that all male children at some time or another wish to have their mothers to themselves, and even wish that the fathers, rivals for first place, die? Not consciously, but in the depths of the psyche.

"The Greek myth seizes on a compulsion which everyone recognizes because he has felt traces of it in himself. Every member of the audience was once a budding Oedipus in fantasy, and this dream-fulfillment played out in reality causes everyone to recoil in horror, with the full measure of repression which separates his infantile from his present state."

He was beginning to remember such emotions in himself, in his early relationship to his mother and father. Now that his father was dead in fact, perhaps part of the reason why he had been so shaken by the death was that guilt was mixed in with sorrow.

"I have found love of the mother and jealousy of the father in my own case, too, and now believe it to be a general phenomenon of early childhood. . ." Might not the same sort of psychological truth lie at the root of Shakespeare's Hamlet, Hamlet being ambivalent in avenging his murdered father's death because he had a secret and unconscious wish for it?

It was long past midnight now. Freud felt a deep weariness

as the result of the intensity of his mental probings. He was on the right track. He was sure of it. But so much more work remained to be done.

Freud's earnings from his medical practice as a neurologist varied greatly as they did with most other physicians. At times the waiting room would be empty for weeks; at others it would be so crowded that he had to work with patients for ten or more hours a day.

For twelve years he had been a Privatdocent; his hopes were directed toward attaining the enviable title of Professor. Due partly to anti-Semitism among the University authorities who could grant the title and due partly to Freud's unpopular theories regarding the sex instinct, his name was repeatedly passed over in favor of younger, more conventionally minded candidates.

Freud pretended not to care but this discrimination, together with his growing sense of scientific isolation, wore upon him. There was one group with which he felt companionship. This was a Jewish lodge, the B'nai B'rith, which he had joined in 1895. Most of his fellow lodge members believed in the ancient Jewish religion and had a deep feeling of pride in there having once been a "nation of Jews." Freud had no strong feelings of a similar kind but he did have a sense of kinship with these Jewish friends, a kinship which he was to describe later as "the clear consciousness of an inner identity, the familiarity of the same psychological structure."

During the summer of 1899, Freud devoted most of his

energies to trying to complete his book on dreams. Much of the writing took place at a family vacation retreat at Berchtesgaden in the Bavarian Alps, a place which was later to be identified with Hitler who appropriated it as his own vacation spot. But when the Freud family was there it was known only as a beautiful German spa, or health resort.

Writing from Berchtesgaden to a friend, Freud described the family's general happiness in a cottage somewhat removed from the crowded tourist quarters, and he lovingly described his children. Anna, he said, was almost "beatified by naughtiness." Martin, his oldest son, was both comical and sensitive, and Oliver was already behaving like an engineer, making plans of the mountains as he did of the transportation system of Vienna.

Freud, despite his concentration on his book, for which he had abandoned strenuous self-analysis for the time, spent many hours with his children, hiking, swimming, or boating on the Königsee, a brilliant lake in a narrow valley between steep, forested mountains.

One occasion the children never forgot was the time "Papa" decided to climb up a steep bank to pick a small, fragrant flower called Kohlroeserl. When he and Martha had first been married he had climbed a similar bank, at some risk, and brought her a wild bouquet. The Alpine roses had been favorites of his and hers ever since. This climb, too, involved risk. Undaunted, he attacked the mountain. He found a bush to hang onto and began triumphantly to pick the blooms.

Suddenly the bush he clung to tore out by the roots. Miraculously, as he fell backward, he managed to do a somersault in air, like a trained diver, and landed safely on his feet.

To his children, this was only further evidence of "Der Papa's" superior abilities. To Freud it was a warning that he was perhaps not quite the mountaineer he had been when he was courting Martha; better that she went without roses than without a husband, her children orphans.

A second episode connected with vacation time in the mountains had a grimmer aspect. Martin and Oliver were fishing on a small lake, the Thumsee, near the famous health resort of Reichenhall. Some men from the resort came by on the lake road and stopped to watch, disapproval on their faces. They began to yell taunts at the young "Israelites" and ordered them to leave. The boys were frightened but remained where they were; finally the hecklers left. When Martin and Oliver returned home they told their father.

Freud's jaw set and his eyes sparked with anger, at the same time that he praised the boys for not retreating. He had never done so. Like his father before him, he told his sons of an incident where he had been challenged and called a "dirty Jew." He had been riding in a stifling hot railway carriage and had opened a window for fresh air. At once, an antagonistic person had yelled at him to close it and had yelled the epithet. Others had joined in. Finally, one man started to climb over the seats toward Freud, threatening to teach him how to behave.

"What did you do then?" Martin asked, the words an echo of Freud's long years ago when he had questioned his father.

"I invited my would-be assailant to come ahead. I was quite prepared to kill him. He tucked his hands into his pockets—perhaps they were suddenly chill—and retreated."

That afternoon Oliver and Martin rowed Freud across the lake on an errand he had to attend to. When they reached the landing place Oliver pointed at a group of persons on the shore. Among them were the men who had badgered them before.

Several women were with the men. As Martin moored the boat both the men and women began to shout. "Jews, go back to your ghettoes where you belong!"

Freud ordered the boys to stay in the boat. He sprang out and marched straight toward the hecklers, his bearded chin thrust out defiantly, eyes blazing, his walking stick swinging from side to side. As he approached the group the hecklers drew back, splitting like water before the keel of a ship. In a moment they had fled, daring only to make a few muttered remarks over their shoulders as they left.

When the boys rowed Freud back across the lake again on completion of his business they felt they were performing a service for a true hero.

Long ago, during his engagement to Martha, he had written to her, "I have often felt as though I had inherited all the defiance and all the passions with which our ancestors defended their Temple and could gladly sacrifice my life for one great moment in history."

The moment by the lake was not a great historical moment, but it required courage. Courage and defiance were qualities Freud needed to protect the "temple" of theory he was building brick by brick in the face of indifference or scorn.

CHAPTER 9

Freud's new book, *The Interpretation of Dreams*, generally considered one of the major and most influential works of our time, appeared at the end of 1899. The motto on the title page is a quotation from Vergil's *Aeneid* which, translated, means, "If I cannot stir the gods above, I will move the infernal regions."

Before Freud, the weight of scientific opinion held that dreams could not be interpreted or had no great significance beyond revealing certain physical states in the dreamer which somehow spilled over into consciousness. Freud asserted that dreams were a part of psychic life, being the life of the mind during sleep. Consequently they could be studied by psychological techniques and their often mysterious language in the form of symbols and images translated into meaning. No dream was meaningless. A diligent searcher into the meanings could gain a better knowledge of a patient's hidden problems and thereby be in a position to provide more intelligent treatment. He himself had successfully treated patients other doctors had despaired of, by interpreting the dream symbols and presenting their significance to the patient.

Basic to Freud's whole theory of dreams was his insistence that the content of dreams revealed a wish in the dreamer, even though the wish might be disguised as something not wanted; this usually occurred when the secret wish was so buried or repressed that a person could not face it in his dream.

Beneath the surface images of a dream lay deeper, more meaningful ones which the conscious part of the mind deliberately covered up or repressed like a censor deleting parts of a message. But, like a crafty writer who tries to get past the censor, the unconscious desires were cunning and insistent on expressing themselves, thus causing the common distortions so familiar in the dream process.

Frequently a person, who in daily life seemed devoted to members of the family, might dream of the death of a loved one, a sister clearly visualizing her brother in the tomb. How could such a dream be a wish fulfillment? Freud traced the dream back to childhood rivalry and resentments, and even hatred between siblings, that is, children of the same parents. At times of conflict, a brother or sister might wish that the other had not been born and want the troublesome rival to simply disappear. Since no desire, conscious or unconscious, remained completely lost in the psyche's deep reservoir, such childhood wishes could return in the grown person's dream. Children could also wish for the death of their parents. Men, Freud noticed, tended to dream of their father's death, women of their mother's. These dreams, too, stemmed from an earlier time, revealing the competitiveness even in little children for the chief place in the life of the parent of the opposite sex. The unconscious was amoral, indifferent to what society considered right or wrong, good or bad.

Dreams also provided wish fulfillment in more obvious ways. They were the guardians of sleep, welling up from the unconscious to provide the dreamer with imaginary satisfactions that were denied him in reality. A crippled person might dream of being a famous athlete, a coward of winning a medal for bravery, a poor man of being rich—demonstrating the truth underlying the common saying, "I couldn't have imagined anything better even in my wildest dreams."

Secret desires, not acceptable by a person's conscience or by conventional social standards, also found satisfaction in dreams. A woman who was normally prudish might dream of walking naked in a crowd without feeling any embarrassment. Such a dream, Freud theorized, was one of a state of childish innocence when there had been no embarrassment about being dandled by a nurse, mother or father in a naked state, or running about freely without the restriction of clothes. It was like a return to a paradise of the kind depicted in the story of Adam and Eve who also were without shame in their nakedness before they ate the fruit of the "tree of knowledge of good and evil" and so learned to be ashamed. Or, a stolid businessman with very correct ideas of behavior might dream of having a love relationship with someone other than his wife, someone he actually yearned for, but could not admit it to himself.

But how could nightmares fit into the pattern of dreams being guardians of sleep or the means of satisfying a wish? This did not change the dream's essential character, Freud said; it was only that the dream had failed to achieve its purpose. A nightmare or anxiety dream usually woke the sleeper before the repressed wish behind the dream could outwit the censor and come to complete fulfillment. It was as if a night watchman who was to protect the dreamer was forced to rouse him in order to ward off threatening danger. Although anxiety was the direct opposite of a wish, said Freud, the opposites lay very near to each other in association and actually coincided in the unconscious.

Freud recognized two main parts of every dream. The surface part of the dream, the most obvious and accessible, he called the manifest dream. Under or within that was the hidden or latent dream with its cargo of suggestion and symbol which could only be revealed by interpretation.

Much of Freud's book dealt with the symbols in dreams which after long study of myths, primitive rites, legends and history, he found to be mainly phallic, or sexual in origin. Some symbols, such as landscapes, ships, boxes, water, seemed always to represent the female gender. Towers, pipes, spears, snakes, stood for the male. Much of the dream material came out of infantile experiences. Symbols were disguises for a reality which the dreamer could not face easily, whether the reality involved sexual desires or other desires which conflicted with a person's good opinion of himself.

Freud's book marked the beginning of a new era, one that is often called the "Freudian Age." *The Interpretation of Dreams,* a monumental undertaking and a defiant one in the face of theories then held, is generally considered Freud's major work. But the majority of the professional critics derided the book when it appeared. One said it was no better than the cheap dream books found in cooks' pantries or in a gypsy fortuneteller's bag. Mostly, the book was ignored. It took eight years to sell the six hundred copies which were printed.

Long after it was published, Freud smilingly told an American psychoanalyst, Ernest Jones, who was to write a three-volume biography of him, "It seems to be my fate to discover only the obvious: that children have sexual feelings, which every nursemaid knows; and that night dreams are just as much a wish fulfillment as day dreams."

What was obvious to Freud was not obvious to the readers of 1900. They were not only disparaging but most were indignant at Freud's attributing sexual feelings and impulses to children. In the face of opposition and indifference, Freud clung to his belief in the importance of his insights into the unconscious, that part of the mental process of which one is not directly aware. For years he had worked in growing isolation and though he suffered from intellectual loneliness, he had developed a firm independence of other people's judgment. But he was saddened to realize that even his old friend

Fliess could no longer be counted on for understanding or sympathy. Fliess was involved in very special theories of his own which became increasingly specialized and even mystical. Freud, out of loyalty, tried to go along with some of Fliess's ideas but the friendship was losing its spontaneity and warmth. Freud clung to it as long as he could, but as with Breuer, he foresaw that the relationship was dying and would never again be what it had been.

He could waste no time on regrets. New ideas were rushing in upon him, new books and pamphlets to be written, lectures, study, a world of continuing exploration.

Lines of age were appearing in his face. His children were growing rapidly. Around him the household, under Martha's capable hands, continued in its regular pattern. Minna, witty and bookish, provided intellectual companionship for him. He had not yet become a Professor and he was still practicing patience in his search for ways to deal with the various forms of neuroses which turned up on his office couch.

From childhood on, Freud had yearned to visit Rome because of its associations with his early hero Hannibal. Yet, he held back from going to the city because of an inner resistance; this he finally overcame through four years of intense self-analysis. In September of 1901 he entered Rome with a sense of triumph and spent twelve unforgettable days in the city. Like other tourists he visited the museums, cathedrals and ancient sites, and tossed a coin into the fountain, Fontana di Trevi; according to tradition, anyone who threw a coin there was bound to return to Rome. More than anything else on this trip Freud was stirred by seeing Michelangelo's powerful statue of Moses. He was to return to the statue again and again in later years until finally he would write a book about its significance to him, *Moses and Monotheism,* the last completed book he was ever to write.

In September, 1904, Freud realized another travel goal. On the morning of the 4th, he and his brother Alex stood on a windless hill overlooking the city of Athens. Freud gazed at the amber-colored columns of the Acropolis with a feeling of unreality.

Only one minor incident dimmed Freud's pleasure during his Athenian visit. He had prided himself on his knowledge of Greek, having written his diary in that language as a youth. So when he and his brother stepped into a carriage one day, Freud told the driver, in Greek, to take them to the Hotel Athena.

The driver looked at him blankly.

Freud repeated his instructions but the ancient Greek pronunciation he had learned was incomprehensible to this modern son of Athens. Beaten, Freud humbly took a notebook and pencil and wrote out what he wished to say. Frowning at the script, the driver finally managed to decipher what Freud meant.

"Even Alexander the Great wouldn't be able to make himself understood here now," Freud said to his brother.

"The centuries have been at work," Alex answered.

As they rode along the streets Freud wondered how many

centuries it would take before he would win recognition for his theories, if ever. There were signs, however, that a few men were beginning to read his books and listen to his lectures at the University with some respect. Several were interested enough to join with him each Wednesday night at his home for talk and discussion, listening to what he had to say. As he had once gone to Charcot to learn, a select group of young doctors were coming to him. Max Kahane, Rudolf Reitler, Wilhelm Stekel and Alfred Adler had been the first. Now the group was large enough to have a name, the "Psychological Wednesday Society."

Freud leaned back in the carriage, gazing again toward the remains of the Parthenon on the hill dominating the city. Perhaps the little Society was a seed from which a greater organization, devoted to promoting a Freudian school of psychology, might grow.

In the same year that Freud visited the Acropolis he published *The Psychopathology of Everyday Life,* a book which is ranked next to his book on dreams in importance. In it Freud tried to answer such questions as why persons forget things which it seemed they should be able to remember easily, like the names of persons well-known to them, an important anniversary, even their own birth dates. A husband forgetting to give his wife a gift on the anniversary of their marriage perhaps did not wish to remember it if the marriage was an unhappy one. As for mistakes in speech, surely there was often more than accidental misstatement involved. Slips of the tongue or of the pen could be revealing of a person's true thoughts. When a war correspondent, for instance, wrote of a heavy-drinking general, meaning to call him a "battle-scarred veteran," and instead referred to him as "bottle-scarred," the mistake seemed too pointed to be dismissed as a slip. As for "accidents," a servant might drop a precious vase, not through carelessness but because the servant secretly resented the object or its owner.

Ignorance and clumsiness could be blamed for some errors or accidents but Freud concluded that there was far less of an element of chance in these than had been supposed. Psychological factors, involving guilt, repression and hostility, were constantly at work not only for patients on the analyst's couch but in everyday life.

Many readers could accept the truths delineated in this book, which Freud had deliberately tried to write in a style that would appeal to the public. But two other writings, *Three Essays on the Theory of Sexuality,* and a case history on a young girl patient called "Dora" brought indignant criticism. In the first, Freud wrote that the sexual instinct or hunger, the "libido," was present even in young children. All bodily sensations of a pleasurable nature, or the desire to experience them, he said, were sexual in nature. Thumb-sucking, for example, could be traced back to a sensual satisfaction bound up with the cravings of the libido, being a substitute for the infantile pleasure of nursing at the mother's breast. In adult life the desire for this particular pleasure could find satisfaction in other substitute activities, such as a man's sucking at the tip of a cigar. Whatever outlets the libido energy took, it was a force beginning in infancy, ceasing for a period of "latency" from around four to puberty and then asserting itself strongly again. Even in adulthood the infantile motivations remained, although the adult might be entirely unconscious of why he sought the love objects he did. When, as often happened because of social laws or other obstacles in what Freud called our "antiquated moral system," an individual could not satisfy his or her particular longings toward a certain love object he might "sublimate" these desires. By sublimation one directed his energies toward some other end. An artist frustrated in his yearning for a beautiful woman might appease his longing by doing a portrait of her. A woman unable to find a satisfactory mate, or to have children, might sublimate her desire for physical love or maternity by devoting herself to nursing or a career in social service.

In Freud's case history of the girl Dora he pursued the idea of sexual motivation in ways which shocked a great many of his contemporaries, giving clinical details which seemed "filthy" or "obscene" to outraged critics. They, like the majority of persons, clung to the idea of childhood innocence. Freud did not regard the sexual impulses as evil, anymore than human beings' other instincts. Facts were facts and if one wanted to create a new science of man's behavior, as he did, then facts could not be ignored or glossed over. Man's psyche, he stressed, rested on a physical or organic base.

In his patient, Dora, a hysterical girl given to nervous fits of coughing, Freud had uncovered an abnormally strong tie toward her father plus a conflicting, strong attraction toward a married woman her father was romantically interested in. This fitted in with his theory that all persons had bi-sexual tendencies; the potentiality to be attracted sexually to a person of the same gender, especially if there seemed no way to establish satisfying relations with a member of the opposite sex.

During his analytic sessions now Freud no longer pressed his hand on a patient's forehead to assure the patient that he would find a crucial memory if he kept trying. He knew that if he waited long enough and listened carefully enough he would hear what he needed to know and that the vital things would float to the surface where they could be trapped and investigated. One of the chief ways of finding out what was in the patient's unconscious was to let the patient ramble on freely, one phrase or thought leading to another, in a seemingly patternless sequence called "free association." Underneath the apparently random associations and behind the gestures or tone of voice, Freud had discovered that a pattern often could be found, one which betrayed the patient's basic anxieties.

With Dora, as with other patients, he made use of his study of dreams. He would question them and then suggest ways of reading the dream involved. He pointed out to Dora how certain objects in her dreams were symbols representing other things—a box and a key, for instance, symbolizing female and male physical counterparts. He disclosed to Dora her strong feeling for her father, a feeling which she had fostered in an attempt to cover up her attraction toward the married woman her father was interested in. More, Dora was also attracted to the woman's husband, K.; at the same time she was afraid to give in to the advances he made toward her, advances which had begun when she was only fourteen. She could not bring herself to say yes to K. and yet she did not want to give a flat no. She compromised by losing her voice when Mr. K. would be away on business, or becoming ill, unconsciously hoping that illness would bring him back to her. By illness, too, she hoped to draw her father away from Frau K. and to herself.

None of this was clear to Dora at the beginning of her analysis, and she tried to conceal the truth both from herself and from Freud. Gradually, as the treatment continued, she was forced to recognize, if not to agree with, Freud's interpretation of many of her acts and thoughts. Recognizing the facts in psychoanalysis is one thing; a deep change of attitude, affecting the unconscious itself, is another. Dora had come to Freud only at her father's insistence and she brought with her a battalion of resistances, plus a conviction that her attitudes stemmed from purely moral considerations. As this conviction was stripped from her she balked and quit the treatment after only three months. By quitting, just when Freud hoped most for success, she was seeking revenge not only against his exposing her to herself as she was, but also against Herr K. She had at first shifted her feelings toward her father to Freud; by this shift, called "transference," a patient reshapes a therapist in fantasy to resemble a figure meaningful to his own past or present. Then, taking Freud by surprise, she transferred what she felt toward Herr K. to him and so, by rejecting Freud, rejected also the man who had disturbed her so by his trying to seduce her even though, unconsciously, she half-welcomed the seduction attempts.

Dora did return to Freud sometime later requesting further treatment, but Freud saw that she was not in earnest. She married later but remained handicapped by all her unresolved conflicts. Although he had not had time to "cure" Dora, Freud learned much from the case and used its revelations for the long paper which he published in 1905, *Fragment of an Analysis of a Case of Hysteria*.

In the meanwhile Freud had not ceased laboring over his own self-analysis. In the labyrinth of his own unconscious he found distressing revelations: envy of his half-brothers, jealousy of his father's closeness to his mother, fear of being replaced by later children born to his parents. His anxiety over train travel he interpreted as a childish fear of losing the home he had been used to in Freiberg, but beyond that the fear of being torn from the nourishment of his mother's breast.

Through his exhaustive self-analysis he began to find a new inner peace to replace the moodiness, nervousness and paralyzing inertia that had often troubled him. He became increasingly his own man. Energies which had been dissipated in anxiety were released for channeling his work. Deliberately he closed his ears to the howl of his critics and doggedly pursued the goals of new discovery glimmering in the distance.

CHAPTER 10

Recognition was slow to come. In 1902 through the help of two good friends, the Baron and Baroness Ferstel, Freud secured the title of Associate Professor in the University of Vienna. In 1904 a colleague, Otto Gross, based a paper on Freud's theories of libido, repression and symbolism. That same year another colleague in Dresden described several successes with cases of hysteria and neurosis based on Freud's psychoanalytic method.

In the autumn of 1904 Freud heard from Eugene Bleuler, director of the famous Burghölzli Clinic of Psychiatry in Zurich, Switzerland, that he and his staff were studying psychoanalysis and had been applying it experimentally for a couple of years. The main inspiration for this was Bleuler's chief assistant, a young Swiss named Carl G. Jung.

This was the beginning of an association between Freud

and Jung which was to be one of the most important friendships in the life of either man. Jung was almost twenty years younger than Freud, a tall, broad-shouldered, blue-eyed son of a Protestant minister. He had first been drawn to Freud's theories by reading *The Interpretation of Dreams*. In 1904 he wrote a book of his own, *The Psychology of Dementia Praecox*, which carried Freud's ideas further than had Freud himself, though it relied on the older man's basic approach. The two began corresponding directly in 1906 and in the following year Jung joined the "Psychological Wednesday Society," which was soon to give itself the name of the "Vienna Psycho-Analytical Society."

Other students and doctors joined the movement around the years of 1906 and 1907. There was Max Eitingon, Russian born, finishing his medical studies at Zurich. Karl Abraham, another young man from Zurich who was beginning to practice analysis in Berlin, brought a warm friendliness that promised a long, close attachment to Freud. He became one of Freud's most loyal supporters. Another young man for whom Freud developed a special attachment was Sandor Ferenczi of Budapest. Freud accepted the sunny-tempered Ferenczi as part of the family and often enjoyed his company on family holidays.

Others attracted toward the movement included Dr. Ernest Jones in America, who had begun practicing analysis on his patients, and another American follower, A. A. Brill.

Because the majority of Freud's followers were Jewish, Freud welcomed those who were not. He did not want psychoanalysis labeled as a Jewish movement. This, in part, made him especially enthusiastic about Jung's joining the movement; also, he saw in Jung much of the same vitality and unfettered imagination that existed in himself. Jung responded to Freud with equal enthusiasm and when the two met in February, 1907, Jung considered it the most important meeting of his life.

Around the same time a little "Freud Group" began in Zurich with Jung as its leader. Dr. Jones had come from America to visit in Zurich and he suggested to Jung that some general gathering of all interested in Freud's work should be arranged. Jung agreed. On a Sunday, April 26, 1908, the first "International Psycho-Analytical Congress," as it was finally to be known, met in Salzburg, Austria.

At the head of a long table Freud sat facing the forty-two men gathered on each side. They included representatives from America, Austria, Switzerland, England, Germany and Hungary.

At age fifty-two grayness had crept into Freud's mustache and pointed beard. He had an air of authority and dignity. The brilliant eyes, which Martha had once felt were those of a seer, remained as bright, quick and penetrating as ever.

As Freud began to describe a case history of one of his patients, he thought that he had never felt more vigorous or young in hope. At last, from all over, a body of intelligent, inquiring men had met together looking to him for leadership. He felt both humility and pride as he talked, his low, conversational tone belying the excitement he felt.

After two hours of the case history Freud decided he had better break off, but the interested men insisted that he go on. At one o'clock he finally quit and sat listening to Jung, Jones, Adler, Ferenczi and others speak. Looking at and listening to Jung, Freud believed that in this dynamic, strong-chinned young man he had found a son and heir who would carry on his work.

Others in the group, especially his earliest adherents, were aware of Freud's enthusiasm for the Swiss disciple. Some of them resented it. Why, they asked, should this comparative stranger be singled out for favoritism?

At the end of the day-long Congress a small group gathered around Freud to discuss the possibility of publishing a periodical devoted to psychoanalysis which would be the first of its kind. Freud was delighted at the idea, especially as it would give him a broad outlet for publishing his own writings, and approved whole-heartedly.

The periodical was to be directed by Bleuler and Freud and edited by Carl Jung.

Among Freud's Viennese friends the sparks of suspicion and resentment against the "outsider," Jung, flared with fresh strength. Antagonism which had broken out between Karl Abraham and Jung intensified. Freud was caught between battling factions. Playing the diplomat was a new role for him but he did his best to try to keep peace for the sake of the psychoanalytical movement.

Back at Berggasse 19, Freud continued his life as before, working with the same intensity, devoting long hours to his practice, watching his family grow up. In 1908 he rented extra space in the flat, enlarging his professional quarters. Anna, his youngest child, toward whom he had always felt a special affection, was then thirteen; Mathilde, the oldest was twenty.

On top of his other activities, Freud wrote and received a great many letters. Whenever he went away on a trip he wrote almost daily to his family, his "dear ones." At home he wrote regularly to colleagues and friends. One morning in December, 1908, he received a letter which sent him hurrying to Martha.

To his "beloved old girl," as he now sometimes called her, he excitedly read the letter from Stanley Hall, president of Clark University in Worcester, Massachusetts. It invited Freud to give a course of lectures at the college. Traveling expenses would all be paid and he would receive 3,000 marks, over seven hundred dollars, as a fee.

Martha was as elated as he, although she could not resist reminding him that he had often been critical of certain features of American life, especially the prevalence of bicycles which he professed to detest. He put his arm around her and smiled. "Detest and affection can exist simultaneously in one person, Marty." He held her close a moment, his face against her hair. The tide was definitely turning in his favor at last, even the tide of the Atlantic Ocean, thanks in good measure to Jones and his other American friends.

Freud sent a message to his friend Ferenczi urging him to accompany him on the American journey. Ferenczi responded with enthusiasm and declared that he would at once start to learn English and read all he could about the country of Washington and Lincoln.

Sometime later when Ferenczi was having dinner at the Freud flat, Freud said that what he chiefly wanted to see in the United States was Niagara Falls, and the collection of Cyprian antiquities in New York. There was plenty of time to decide on their itinerary since they had until August to make their plans.

When in June Freud learned that Jung, too, had been invited to lecture at Clark University, he said, "That magnifies the importance of the whole affair," and immediately made plans for Jung, Ferenczi and himself to make the trip together.

They met in Bremen and sailed on the *George Washington* on August 21, 1909.

Freud, coming across his cabin steward during a rest period one day while on board, noticed that the man was hunched over a book. Freud asked what he was reading with such concentration and the steward held up his book. It was Freud's own *The Psychopathology of Everyday Life.*

Sigmund Freud began to get an inkling then of how far his writings had reached into the public mind.

The lectures Freud gave in Massachusetts were delivered in German, without any notes, and were finally published in 1920 as *A General Introduction to Psycho-Analysis.* At the end of the lecture series Clark University conferred an honorary doctor's degree on Freud.

Standing before the crowd to accept this honor Freud's

voice broke slightly as he said, "This is the first official recognition of our endeavors."

In the course of his visit to the United States, Freud met William James, one of the nation's most respected philosophers. Freud invited his new friend to go for a walk with him. James was carrying a briefcase. The two were walking and conversing—James knew the German language well—when James stopped suddenly. Jerkily he asked Freud if he would take his briefcase and go on ahead. He was having an attack of angina, he said; it would be over in a moment.

William James died of a heart attack a year later and Freud realized that James had known when they met how brief his life span was likely to be. He always remembered how James had put an arm around his shoulder, saying, "The future of psychology belongs to your work."

In his *Autobiography*, Freud wrote, "I have always wished that I might be as fearless as he was in the face of approaching death." It was a wish that would be more than fulfilled.

At age fifty-three Freud was still far from death. But, during his visit to Niagara Falls, which was an even grander spectacle than he had anticipated, he had been both amused and jolted by a remark made by the guide. The man had pushed the other sightseers back and told them to let the "old fellow" go first.

Freud arrived back in Vienna on October 2. It was the one place that continued to refuse him respect or honor but it was home, which the sprawling, bustling world of America, for all its hospitality, was not.

CHAPTER 11

Storm clouds blew across the sky, their shadows touching pages of the book open on Freud's desk. Freud read, frowning, then looked out at the darkening day. How sadly different things were now in 1912 for the Psycho-Analytic Association and for his relationship with Carl Jung from what they had first been.

The title of the book stared up at him, *Symbols of the Libido.* Jung's latest work. Jung's latest rebellion against Freud. The libido was not a sexual force, as Freud had stated, Jung argued, but merely a general tension embracing the sum total of vital energies.

"He is the man of the future," Freud had told Ferenczi only a little over a year ago, though even then he had begun to be uneasy over Jung's increasing tendency toward a mystical and religious interpretation of man's unconscious. Still he had persisted in supporting Jung as the leader and president of the Psycho-Analytic Association even in the face of the growing bitterness of the Viennese members' opposition. At times the dissension within the group had broken into outright verbal warfare. Alfred Adler, one of Freud's first advocates, had especially resented the influence of the Swiss Jung. At the same time, Adler, like Jung, had begun to follow an independent course in his own psychological theories, stressing the role of inferiority and superiority complexes in human behavior and rebelling against what he felt was Freud's excessive authority. Adler had deserted the Freudian ranks at last, taking nine adherents with him.

First Adler, Freud thought, taking down a Roman statuette and turning it over and over in his hands, and now the man he had hoped for most as his "Crown Prince," Carl Jung. Only this spring Freud had clung to hope in the face of Jung's saying that Freud's theories on incest wishes, as in the Oedipus complex, were merely fantasies or symbols of other tendencies.

Differences in theory, Freud had told him, need not disturb their personal relationship.

In September Jung had delivered a course of lectures in New York. Reports came to Freud that Jung was disparaging Freud's theories and calling them out of date. Jung himself, on his return, wrote to Freud explaining that he had made the idea of psychoanalysis more acceptable to his American audiences by leaving out the sexual themes. Deeply dismayed, Freud had responded that obviously the theories could be made even more acceptable by leaving out everything an audience might not like.

Remembering, he tapped his fist lightly, impatiently, against the desk. Had he been too much a dictator, as some contended? He had tried to bind the warring groups together, compromising, assuaging, retiring from his own presidency of the Viennese group so that Adler could fill the post. One thing he could not do was to abandon the very heart of his theory. Without the cornerstone of sexual motivation the entire edifice he had built would crash. He had lost friends before because of his loyalty to his own ideas. He had also gained many, including even a Protestant clergyman, Oskar Pfister of Zurich. Facing criticism and even persecution, the "Dear Man of God," as Freud addressed Pfister in his letters, had remained loyal—Abraham, too, and Otto Rank, Ferenczi, Ernest Jones, and Hanns Sachs.

Even so, Freud's heart was heavy. Striving for optimism, he looked ahead to the meeting he, Jung and several other members of the Association would attend next month, in November. Perhaps by talking together he and Jung could narrow the chasm widening between them.

In November the Munich meeting occurred as planned and during a long walk Freud and Jung reached what seemed to be a more harmonious relationship. Jung apologized for certain animosities he had displayed and admitted resentments. Freud gave him a fatherly lecture, mixed with criticism. Jung accepted both in a spirit of contrition.

The two went back to luncheon at the hotel where the

group was meeting, Freud feeling triumphant at having won Jung to him again. In the midst of a discussion with his colleagues Freud suddenly fell to the floor in a faint.

He revived quickly. Ferenczi helped him to a chair, a strange expression on his face. Ferenczi said nothing until later when they were alone. Then he asked Freud if he recalled a previous fainting attack which had occurred when Jung was present. "It happened when the three of us were setting out to America, remember?"

Freud nodded. On that occasion, too, he had won a small victory over Jung, persuading Jung who never drank liquor to celebrate with some wine.

Trying to analyze these fainting attacks, Freud traced them back to a death wish he had had as a small child against his infant brother, Julius. When Julius had actually died an unconscious guilt had been set up in Sigmund. Now, even in this trifling victory over a younger rival such as Jung, the emotion of long ago exploded like a delayed time bomb, sending him into a faint.

However briefly victorious Freud may have felt, the peace between him and Jung did not last. Freud made the mistake of saying that there was a resemblance between one of Jung's theories and one of Adler's.

Stung by the suggestion that his school of thought owed anything to Adler's, Jung wrote an angry letter to Freud. In it he made a slip of the pen, saying ". . . not even Adler's companions think that I belong to your group." What he had intended to say was that no one thought he belonged to Adler's group. When Freud pointed out this slip as being further proof of Jung's hidden antagonism, Jung wrote again more explosively than before, accusing Freud of wanting to keep all of his pupils in infantile dependency.

Freud wrote a mild answer to this letter but he never mailed it. From then on, he decided, the only letters he would write to Jung would be strictly on business matters. The personal relationship was over. Freud realized that he and Jung were moving in entirely different directions and the Psycho-Analytical Association, of which Jung was still president, would be torn apart.

In April, 1914, Jung resigned his presidency and then completely withdrew from the Association. With him went his Swiss colleagues.

Jung was hailed as one who was bringing sanity back to psychoanalysis by throwing out Freud's "obscene" concentration on sexual topics. Those who had called Freud's work pornographic, something to be dealt with not by science but by the police, were encouraged to renew their attacks. Men like Pastor Pfister were in danger of being dismissed from their pulpits because of allegiance to Freud. Ernest Jones had been forced to resign a neurological appointment in London for pursuing Freud's method of analysis. In Budapest Sandor Ferenczi had been stopped from reading a paper on Freudian theory, before the Medical Society there. "Freud's work is filth," the assembled doctors said. And in the United States, which had honored him with a lofty degree, Freud had now been called a "typical Viennese libertine," indifferent to ordinary standards of decency or morals.

One group of personal friends stood fast. Like a bodyguard they ringed themselves around Freud, calling themselves the Committee. The idea of such a committee had begun with Ferenczi and Jones in 1912. The first five members were Ernest Jones, Sandor Ferenczi, Otto Rank, Hanns Sachs and Karl Abraham. Later Max Eitingon was invited to join.

When the first five met with Freud in the summer of 1913, Freud gave each an antique Greek stone engraving from his collection; each stone was subsequently mounted in a gold ring. Freud himself had long worn a similar ring engraved with the head of Jupiter.

To Freud this banding together of loyal supporters was desirable for more than his personal gratification. Jung's and Adler's drawing away from the movement he had started was a danger signal. Psychoanalysis had been his creation, and his alone. Who could claim to understand it better than he? He must guard the citadel and explain its ground plan and turrets to all. The important thing then, for him and for the Committee, was to draw up a solid description of what Freudian psychoanalysis was and the techniques used in it.

With Jung and Adler in mind he wrote, "Men are strong as long as they represent a strong idea; they become powerless when they oppose it. Psycho-analysis will survive this loss and gain new adherents in place of these others." In essay after essay he outlined and defended and explained precisely what his own school of psychoanalysis was, emphasizing the basic premises and developing new ideas which modified or extended earlier ones he had held.

One of the pleasant highlights of the year 1912 was nineteen-year-old Sophie's engagement to a Hamburg photographer, Max Halberstadt. Mathilde had been married three years before to a young Viennese, Robert Hollitscher.

"Baby" Anna was now seventeen, a deeply serious, studious girl much interested in her father's work. She, it appeared, would be the one to follow in her father's footsteps. Martin, with a degree as a doctor of law, was serving his legal apprenticeship; Oliver was preparing himself for a career in mathematical engineering, Ernst in architecture.

In spite of the critics and opposition of certain medical groups, or dissension within the ranks of Freud's own followers, life at the Freud flat followed a comparatively serene pattern. And the name of Sigmund Freud was one that increasingly had to be reckoned with; he was emerging at last from the isolation he had experienced for so long.

Meanwhile, war clouds were gathering over Central Europe, one national power jostling another or threatening armed hostilities as a means of settling age-old rivalries. Freud followed political developments with no special interest. Then on June 28, 1914, the news came that the heir to the throne of Austria, the Archduke Franz Ferdinand, and his wife, had been assassinated in Sarajevo. Serbian conspirators were blamed for the deed. To many, it seemed this was the spark which would set off a general war.

Freud, too, felt apprehensive. Anna, who had made plans to go to England for a couple of months, faced the possibility that her plan would be frustrated because of the dangers involved. However, after the first few days of alarm following the assassination things seemed to settle back to normal again and Freud decided it would be all right for Anna to leave. She would be safe in England with relatives and her heart was set on the trip. In early July he saw her off on a train to Hamburg where she would spend a few weeks visiting Sophie and her husband before going on to England.

It was after Anna reached England that Austria delivered an ultimatum to Serbia which resulted in Austria's declaring war and bombing Belgrade, now the capital of Yugoslavia. The first World War had begun.

Both Freud and Martha were concerned for Anna, as well as for their sons who were of an age to be called into active military service. Freud felt anxiety for Austria itself. He had not believed that war would come, and now it was here with its threat to physical life and to the life of the mind. What would happen to that special child of his intellect, psychoanalysis and the International Psycho-Analytical Association if other countries intervened in the war, a prediction made by many people.

By the first of August, 1914, the predictions came true. Germany sided with Austria-Hungary; Russia took the side of Serbia. France supported Russia, fearful that the Germans would seize control of Central Europe. England teetered on the edge of a decision but finally joined with France, Russia and Serbia in a combination of nations known as the Allies. Other nations, too, were being drawn into the conflict.

Suddenly, as though shattered by a bomb, Freud's world was in chaos. Although he was a pacifist at heart, he was at first caught up in the war fever. Using the language of his own profession, he declared, "All my libido is given to Austria-Hungary." Forgotten was the neglect, the abuse and the lack of respect that Austria, and Vienna in particular, had accorded him.

Through the help of friends, Freud managed to bring Anna home from England. Martin was one of the early volunteers in the war, leaving his legal apprenticeship in the beautiful city of Salzburg, in that part of the Austrian Alps where the Freud family had spent so many happy summer days. When Freud received notice of Martin's enlistment he was torn between pride and concern. The latter expressed itself in his sending Martin money to buy himself some extra warm clothing. "I dreamt that I saw you in a thick, fur-lined waistcoat," he wrote. "Frankly, so far as you are concerned, I am more afraid of epidemics, whose acquaintance can be made very easily just now, than of enemy bullets."

Freud's military fervor faded before the onslaught of bloodshed and brutalities war brought, but as a loyal Austrian he hoped for a German and Austrian victory. War brought wretchedness not only in material but in spiritual conditions. Added to his growing depression over the conflict was the news that his half-brother Emmanuel had been killed in a railway accident in November. Although Emmanuel was eighty-one years old and their lives were greatly separated by distance, Freud was jolted by his death.

It was a sad Christmas but the privations and sufferings of the people in Central Europe had barely begun. Freud's young colleagues, Ferenczi, Rank and Sachs, were called up for military service. And by 1915, Oliver and Ernst were both in uniform. When Italy took up arms, Ernst was sent to the Italian front. Oliver, a graduate engineer, was helping to build tunnels, barracks, and bridges for the military. Anna, who in the summer of 1915 was staying with Freud's eighty-year-old mother at a spa in the Salzkammergut, worried, "How am I going to take the place of six children all by myself?"

It was a period of deep anxiety for Freud, and loneliness, though he told a correspondent, Lou Andreas-Salomé, "I am writing from an idyll which we, my wife and I, have defiantly and stubbornly created for ourselves. . ." He felt that he was once again the only person left to fight for psychoanalysis. Ferenczi made a few quick visits to Vienna during furloughs from the army; otherwise Freud had to depend mostly on correspondence to keep in touch with his friends. Letters from sympathetic colleagues, such as those from Dr. James Putnam, Professor of Neurology at Harvard, Jones in England and Abraham in Germany helped to make him feel that his movement had not been destroyed by bullets and national hatreds. Anxious for the fate of scientific journals he had helped to found, Freud abandoned writing books to concentrate on keeping the magazines alive in the face of paper shortages.

Food and fuel were in short supply. Freud's study was often so cold that he wrote with numb fingers. Toward the end of 1917, he noticed that something was seriously wrong with his mouth and jaw. He had run out of cigars and was, in his own words, bad-tempered and tired. He noticed that his heartbeats were more rapid than normal. This was followed by a painful swelling in his palate. A patient brought him a supply of cigars and after he had smoked one the swelling subsided.

Smoking was his medicine, he decided, but again, as earlier, he believed he would not live long. There was only grim resignation left, he confided to his friend Abraham. "My mother will be eighty-three this year. . .I sometimes think I shall feel a little freer when she dies, for the idea that she might have to be told that I have died is a terrifying thought."

Despite the war, the Psycho-Analytical Association had its Fifth Congress in September, 1918, in Budapest, and was the first such congress to have representatives of any government present.

In 1919 Freud was made a full professor at the University of Vienna, but he felt this was an empty title as it did not give him a seat on the Board of the Faculty.

Grimly, Freud and Martha struggled through the wartime period. When the end of the bloody contest came, with victory for the Allies substantially aided by the United States' entry into the war, they could scarcely believe their good fortune; all three of their sons returned.

Lost, however, were most of Freud's savings, due to high prices and decrease in value of money. Martha's brother Eli sent money from America to try to help but this was only a temporary stopgap. Freud had to depend on his medical practice for his main support and no one in war-wrung Austria had money for psychoanalysis. His only hope was to obtain patients from England and America. American and English currency retained its basic value.

With the help of Ernest Jones and others, Freud began to acquire foreign patients. Analyzing these English-speaking clients, or teaching American and English students who wanted to learn Freud's methods of analysis, was especially hard work for Freud who had never felt at home in the English language.

He had several offers to arrange for him to migrate to the United States, Canada or England. He refused and wrote to Jones, "I will stay at my post as long as I reasonably can."

CHAPTER 12

Even though 1920, like the other years following the end of the war, was grim, life went on much as before. Martin Freud was married and had two children. Sophie also had two. Freud and his colleagues arranged for another congress of the International Psycho-Analytical Association. This, the sixth, was held in The Hague, Holland. Among the fifty-seven guests sat Anna Freud.

That year Anna was to wear a new ring on her finger but it was not a wedding ring. It was a replica of the rings worn by the Committee which had banded around Freud. Anna was twenty-four, holder of a schoolteacher's degree, and dedicated to her father's work. Although the Committee members had continued through war, poverty and strife to be Freud's mainstay, even to smuggling food and cigars to him, none was closer to him than Anna. She was an intense, devoted committee in herself, he thought.

Only three other women were to be honored by receiving a similar ring: Ernest Jones's wife; a beautiful and intellectual former student of Freud's, Lou Andreas-Salomé who counted Tolstoy, Rodin, and Rilke among her friends; and Princess Marie Bonaparte, sister-in-law of the King of Greece. For Martha, the only romantic love of Freud's adult life, the wedding ring he had given her years before was all the symbol of devotion needed.

In the statue-crowded study overlooking the Berggasse shops, Freud continued his writing and researches. Work was as important to him as daily bread. "I could not contemplate with any sort of comfort a life without work," he said.

He and Martha needed all the comfort they could find at the beginning of 1920. In January, Freud lost his beloved friend, Anton von Freund who was a wealthy brewer of Budapest, to cancer. On the day of von Freund's funeral news came announcing that Sophie was seriously ill at her home in Hamburg. She had contracted influenzal pneumonia, the disease which had run rampant after the war.

Unbelieving, racked by anxiety for their beautiful "Sunday child" as they called Sophie, Freud and Martha were forced to sit helpless and wait for further news as they were unable to get a train out of Vienna to Germany.

The news came on January 25, a telegram to tell them that Sophie, only twenty-six, was dead. Martha was too prostrated by the shock to try to reach Hamburg by whatever means and

Freud would not leave her to grieve alone. So the two stayed in Vienna during the funeral, leaving it up to Ernst and Oliver, who were both in Berlin, to take their place. Mathilde and her husband Robert Hollitscher who lived in Vienna, went later to help Sophie's husband decide what to do about the two young children left motherless.

Writing to his friend Ferenczi about his loss, Freud said that as an unbeliever in a personal, supernatural power, he had no one to accuse and no one to complain to about the deep hurt of his daughter's death. Duty and the "dear, lovely habit of living," he hoped, would help him go on as before.

The habit of living, for Freud, meant going on with his work. About a month after Sophie's death, Freud had the satisfaction of seeing the Berlin Policlinic open, a training center for analysts which was the first of its kind. Personal pride entered in, too, as it was his son Ernst who designed the arrangement of the building. Hanns Sachs came from Switzerland to assist in the teaching, and from Vienna came Theodore Reik who was later to become well known in America for his own writings on psychoanalysis.

Another important project to Freud at this time was promoting success of a publishing house specializing in books on psychoanalysis, the *Internationaler Psychoanalytischer Verlag*. He, Ferenczi, von Freund and Rank had been the original directors when the *Verlag* was founded in 1919. Von Freund had left a bequest of $500,000, but inflation reduced the value of the money greatly so that Freud and his friends had to struggle constantly to keep the publishing firm in existence. They managed until the Nazis finally confiscated the *Verlag* some twenty years later. Small, wiry Otto Rank worked like a giant to keep up with editorial and managerial details. Later, when the press was floundering, Martin left his law practice to try to save it.

To Freud the *Verlag* represented a channel through which he could publish what he wanted, independent of outside editors' whims or demands. Although some of his friends assumed that the stresses of war, plus his increasing age, meant that his creative energies were spent, essays and books continued to pour from Freud's pen. Anthropology, history, superstition and myth were among the fields he investigated. His ideas grew even bolder and he let his imagination, which he had kept in stricter harness in younger days, rove freely over the whole field of the human psyche. He modified or expanded earlier convictions. In a paper called *Supplements to the Theory of Dreams* he extended his wish fulfillment theory to include unconscious wishes that did not bring pleasure but self-punishment to satisfy a nagging conscience.

There was a part of the mind, he decided, which operated beyond what he called the "pleasure principle." In this latter, the mental processes were concerned with avoiding pain or anxiety, the aim being pleasure and escape from painful tension. But this search for pleasure was modified by the demands of reality, or the "reality principle"—the conditions or facts met with in the outside world. The pursuit of pleasure in defiance of physical costs or moral standards could bring about a sense of guilt which, in turn, resulted in self-punishment, even a secret wish for death.

Man's mind was a battleground between opposing drives. On the one hand there were the instinctual drives typified by the sexual instinct. The sex drive, named for Eros, the god of love, found itself often in conflict with the "ego." Ego, Freud originally described as the non-sexual part of ourselves concerned with self-preservation and self-assertion; to it lay the task of gaining control over the demands of the instincts, the innate, involuntary impulses in ourselves.

Freud tended to think in dualistic terms, that is, in terms of one thing opposed or counterbalanced by another: life against death, Eros versus the ego, consciousness against the unconscious, pain against pleasure, self-destruction versus self-preservation. Fact and theory revolved in his mind, and he began to force his "scientific" system to the verge of philosophy and metaphysics as he extended his concepts. Groping, following uncharted roads through the human psyche, Freud tried to draw up a guide map of man's emotional and mental life that others could follow toward a deeper understanding of why we act as we do. Nothing was simple and nothing was random or meaningless.

He had gone far beyond a laboratory microscope and dissection of nerve tissues, but his aim was still to establish psychoanalysis as a science. Nevertheless, psychoanalysis, as practiced by students and colleagues he had trained, seemed often more an art than a science. The analyst who operated by keen intuition or discerning hunch might surpass the drudge who memorized Freud's lectures by heart but lacked a natural talent for the work. Freud himself had depended much on intuition and imaginative insight. Yet analytic technique was supremely important. Jung and Adler had developed new techniques and therefore their understanding of cases differed from Freud's and, in his opinion, also differed from the clinical realities they were investigating, due to inadequate knowledge.

The life of the mind had an organic base, Freud had long stressed. In him, too, the organic was at work. On a February morning in 1923, Freud stood in front of a mirror in his and Martha's bedroom, studying his own reflection. Outwardly he looked healthy enough but once again, there was something very wrong with his palate and jaw; he could feel a strange growth there on the right side.

Martha happened into the room and looked at him curiously. Was there something wrong? she asked.

He dodged the question by saying lightly that he was only thinking about how old they both were growing. There was no need to alarm her, Freud thought. As it was she was worried enough by other matters, including her concern over Sophie's young children. Heinerle, the youngest, was staying in Vienna now with Mathilde and her husband. The four-year-old boy had won both Freud's and Martha's hearts.

Freud rubbed his jaw, sighed and turned away. Perhaps another cigar would help assuage the increasing discomfort there.

By April he realized that more than the "medicine" of cigar

smoke was needed. He decided to consult a nose and throat specialist without saying anything to his family.

The doctor's verdict was blunt. "You'll have to have the growth operated on, Herr Professor. However, it won't require your being hospitalized as it will be a slight matter."

Freud arranged to have the operation done on April 20 at the hospital's out-patient clinic. He left his flat in the morning, saying only that he had an errand to do, planning to return home in a few hours.

The operation did not turn out to be as minor as the doctor had predicted. Shortly after the growth was removed, the ring of the telephone at Berggasse 19 interrupted Martha's chores. Hurrying to answer it, she was told that her husband was at the clinic and would have to spend the night there.

Shocked and distraught Martha signaled to Anna to come and take over the telephone.

"Bring something for Dr. Freud to sleep in," the nurse at the clinic told Anna. He had lost a good deal of blood, she went on, so that the doctor wanted him to stay for the night.

Anna clutched the receiver. Yes, she promised. She and her mother would come at once.

At the clinic, Martha and Anna found Freud sitting on a kitchen chair in the out-patient department, blood stains on his clothing. He was not able to speak and only shook his head when they pressed for an explanation.

Dr. Hajek, the surgeon, appeared and explained what had happened. There were no single rooms vacant, he said, but a bed had been prepared in a room with only one other occupant. The other occupant turned out to be a huge-headed dwarf, with a smile that suggested that his mentality was as dwarfed as his body.

Martha and Anna stayed with Freud until the lunch hour when they were required to leave according to the hospital rules. In the interval while they were gone Freud had another attack of severe bleeding. He tried to ring the room bell to summon help but the bell was out of order. It was the dwarf who rushed down the corridors to bring help.

Anna spent the night at the hospital, hovering near her father. The growth which had been removed was found to be cancerous but Freud was not told.

Little Heinerle, the grandson, had his tonsils removed about the same time as Freud had his jaw operation. When grandfather and grandson met for the first time after their separate operations, Heinerle said, "I can already eat crusts. Can you too?"

Freud, smiling, shook his head, and lifted the child into his lap.

Less than two months later, this favorite grandchild was dead of miliary tuberculosis. It was the only time in Freud's adult life that anyone saw him shed tears.

In the same year, 1923, Freud published his book *The Ego and the Id*. The ego he described as the essential "I" in an individual, the part of the mind involved with reason and choice, developed by primitive man in his relations with the external world. Contrasted to the ego was the "id," the obscure, inaccessible part of personality containing everything

147

inherited, the instincts, passions, and primitive impulses. There, in this psychic storehouse, the ceaseless energy of the libido with its blind appetite for pleasure throbbed like a dynamo. Over and above the ego stood the "super-ego" like a supervisor in charge of ideals and aims, saying, "You must not," or "You must."

All three terms refer not to actual physical realities but to psychic organizations within all individuals. Neurosis, Freud said, resulted from a struggle between the demands of the id and those of the ego. Psychosis, extreme mental illness, was caused by a disturbed relation between the ego and the outer world. Even in persons with no mental or emotional illness the struggle went on, the id striving blindly and with no awareness of right and wrong to have its way against the ego trying to obey the laws of the world and civilization.

In the late summer of the year Freud stood once again in his beloved Rome. Anna was with him. It was for her sake that he had come, so that he could have the pleasure of showing her about the city. Her enthusiasm and delight in everything around her almost made him forget the pain that again gnawed at his upper jaw and the major operation scheduled on his return to Vienna.

During the time he and Anna spent in Rome he received a clipping from a Chicago newspaper which said he was slowly dying, had given up his work and had transferred his pupils to Rank.

"If I only die slowly enough," he told Anna, "I could live to be a hundred! In the meantime, I hold to Bernard Shaw's advice in *The Doctor's Dilemma*—'Don't try to live forever, you will not succeed!' "

On October 4 and 11 an oral surgeon, Professor Hans Pichler, performed Freud's operation in two stages. Painful and complicated though the surgery was, Freud endured the ordeal under a local anesthetic. From the sanatorium, while convalescing, he wrote a brief report of the surgery to his mother. A kind of magnified denture had been designed for him to wear in order to replace the malignant portions of his palate and jaw which had been removed; but about that he wrote only that it would take him some time to grow used to it. Actually, the contraption which he labeled "the monster" was, and continued to be, a source of great discomfort for the rest of his life. Even with Anna's help—he insisted on her being his only nurse—he often had trouble inserting or removing it. Aside from the painful irritation it caused, the device affected his speech. He who had always spoken with precise diction, in pleasant tones, now found his voice thick and slurred. Eating, too, became such a trial, as he had difficulty in opening his mouth, that he preferred not to dine in company. Due to recurring infections his hearing also was impaired so that he became almost entirely deaf on the affected side. However, work he would and must. He simply changed the position of his analyst's couch and moved his chair in which he sat listening to a patient, so that his good ear could take over the job.

At the very beginning of his illness he had made a pact with Anna. No matter what happened, or what agonies might be involved for either of them, there should be no sentimentality or emotionalism. She should treat him as if she were a professional nurse or doctor. Partly because of his own stoicism, partly because of her dedication and courage, the pact was never broken though Freud was to have some thirty more operations on his jaw. Some were comparatively minor, as forms of treatment, but none were without their painful aspects.

The news of Freud's major jaw operation tended to soften some Viennese hearts toward him so that the City Council unbent so far as to bestow on him, on his 68th birthday, a special honor similar to our American custom of giving a distinguished guest the "key to the city." Authors Romain Rolland and Stefan Zweig came to visit him. Beyond Europe Freud's fame was spreading to the extent that he was invited by the powerful Hearst news syndicate to come to the United States to psychoanalyze two young murderers, Leopold and Loeb, offering any sum Freud named.

Freud stayed "at his post," his offices in the building where he had spent so many productive, mind-soaring years. Though his interest in the human psyche dominated his activity, he was increasingly concerned with the political and social life of mankind and with what it meant to be a Jew in an atmosphere of animosity and hatred.

To Rolland he wrote, ". . . if in the course of evolution we don't learn to divert our instincts from destroying our own kind, if we continue to hate one another for minor differences and kill each other for petty gain, if we go on exploiting the great progress made in the control of natural resources for our mutual destruction, what kind of future lies in store for us?"

CHAPTER 13

Freud, seventy years old on May 6, 1926, sat in the drawing room going through the letters and telegrams of congratulation on his birthday. There were so many that Anna and Martha were kept busy trying to sort them and keep them in some kind of order.

Anna shuffled through a newly arrived batch of envelopes, reading the return addresses aloud. "George Brandes, Bleuler, Romain Rolland, Yvette Guilbert and Albert Einstein."

Freud took the letters and telegrams into his own hands. Beside his chair were copies of laudatory articles about him which had been published in the Vienna newspapers and in Germany. Once he had dreamed of fame. Now that it was here, how little difference it made. Yet it was undeniably pleasant to receive greetings and well wishes from all over the world, and especially from a brilliant theoretical physicist like

Einstein who had won the Nobel Prize in 1921. He had heard rumors that he himself was being proposed for the prize.

Tapping his finger against an article published by his friends of B'nai B'rith, he said with humor, "If somebody abuses me, I can defend myself to the limit. But this praise —against it I'm defenseless. My Jewish friends are treating me like a national hero, even though I shun the synagogue and have spent my life trying to destroy their and other men's illusions."

He had not been alone in delivering a blow to man's illusions and pride. Copernicus had displaced man from his belief that he was the center of the universe. Darwin had destroyed the belief that man was a special creation separate from the animal world. And now he, Freud, had spent a lifetime showing that man was not even the master of his own mind.

He looked at the paper mountain of correspondence around him. Tomorrow the members of the Committee would appear here to deliver their congratulations in person, all except his old friend Abraham who had died the year before. "A man of upright life and free of stain," Freud had quoted from Horace in his obituary of Abraham.

One of the hazards of living a long life, he reflected, was having to say a final farewell to one's friends. Fleischl-Marxow had led the list in 1891. Then had come Josef Breuer. Tomorrow he would say farewell to the Committee members in a different way. He would tell them that they must carry on the psychoanalytical movement by themselves. A semi-invalid such as he, forced by "the monster" in his mouth and his failing heart to remain close to surgeon and nurse could no longer bear the main burden. Above all, he thought, he must ask his friends to bear witness to posterity of the comradeship they had shared. There had been disagreements but at the core was love and loyalty.

"I have had wonderful friends," he said. "What more can a man attain?"

Although Freud on this birthday took a vacation from his work for four days, to give himself to the Committee and his many other guests, he had by no means retired from active medical practice or from his writing. Neither physical suffering nor age could destroy the fertility of his mind. Especially important to him in these years was the controversy over the proper qualifications of persons doing psychoanalytical work. He did not want psychoanalysis to be a tool only of medically trained doctors. Many lay persons had a natural talent for analysis; after the World War a number of non-medical analysts had begun to practice in Vienna. Rank was one of the first. Now Theodore Reik and his own Anna were following suit. Men and women in London, too, were entering the field, training to be analysts without a doctor's degree. In America the opposition of the medical society was strong. His longtime American champion, Brill, was threatening to break off relations with Freud if the accepting Viennese attitude toward lay analysis continued. Freud took time off from the controversy and his work only for the jaw operations which were becoming a regular feature of his life, or for recuperative vacations in the healing atmosphere of the mountains.

In old age, a new pleasure was added to Freud's life—dogs. It was the Greek princess, Marie Bonaparte, who gave him his first chow. One especially, named Jofi, became Freud's constant companion. Jofi never left Freud's side, not even when he treated patients. She would lie motionless near his chair, waiting while her master conducted his analyses. At the end of the analytic hour, Jofi would yawn to signify that the time was up, being more reliable than his own watch.

As a personal companion, Jofi provided a quiet affection that Freud found therapeutic. Thrusting his fingers into her soft fur, stroking the reddish brown ears, he could find a momentary distraction from the physical suffering that afflicted him through most of the day and night. If a groan escaped him, Jofi was sympathetic without being upset. Even Martha, whose Orthodox background had tended to make her think of dogs as unclean animals, never considered as family pets, enjoyed Jofi and the other chows Freud assembled around him.

Though pets were a solace, they could not provide the help Freud needed in other ways. In 1929 the *Verlag* reached one of its periodic financial crises. Marie Bonaparte volunteered to save it from bankruptcy and other persons sent donations, including an anonymous patient of Freud's who gave $1,000. It was not the first time that grateful patients had voluntarily given money to Freud and his projects, a form of appreciation that meant much to him since the aim of psychoanalysis was essentially that of healing. Philosophy and theory aside, Freud strove to be a doctor to the sufferers on his analyst's couch. His method was essentially a dictate, "Know thyself," and thereby be healed.

The psychoanalytic technique Freud had developed had not changed drastically from that of his early, experimental days. Sitting at the head of the couch, out of sight of the patient (he had told Martha he could not stand being stared at eight hours a day), he encouraged the patient to talk freely about whatever entered his or her mind, no matter how trivial it might seem. From the seemingly random method of free association he discovered clues to the basic conflicts in the patient. With his help the patient himself would begin to find traumatic events or desires buried in his unconscious rising to consciousness. Psychic traumas were the result of experiences which left a hidden scar in the unconscious, often the result of frightening events in early childhood. Only by bringing such "forgotten" experiences to the surface of consciousness could a patient deal with them.

One of the essential elements in a successful analysis, Freud had learned, was the event he called "transference." In the course of treatment the patient would begin to transfer to the analyst the emotions he had felt toward love-objects or hate-objects of his childhood, usually a parent. Breuer had been the object of a love transference in the case of Anna O. Freud too had had the same experience many times. A woman patient might think she had fallen in love with him, substituting him for some other forgotten or unsatisfactory love-object in her life. It took tact and forbearance to make her eventually see that she was only transferring her emotions in an attempt to avoid her true impulses. Or she could develop hostility. Male patients, too, could develop deep feelings of affection or dependence toward the analyst. Or if they had been dominated by a father whom they secretly resented, they might project the hostility onto the doctor. Always such transferences revealed much of the patient's hidden erotic life. Where the hostility or resentment was too great or where no transference took place, there was little hope of therapy. This happened, particularly, with deeply psychotic or "insane" patients.

Freud added new words, or new meanings for old words, to the language. "Fixation" was one, describing how some individuals become fixed at a certain point in their development and unable to progress beyond that. Some always remained infants emotionally, clinging to their infantile self-love. Some might be caught in the Oedipus stage, a boy fixed in his attachment to his mother, the girl unable to love any man except her father. (Since Freud's time the latter situation has been called the Electra complex.) Such a person, as an adult, would tend to see as a mate someone resembling the loved parent.

All persons, Freud said, had both masculine and feminine elements in their natures in varying degrees and therefore had bi-sexual tendencies, the capacity to be attracted to either sex. Homosexuals, however, tended to be attracted only to persons of their own gender. Such a situation commonly existed in pre-adolescence where boys preferred the company of other boys, and girls clung together. When such a preference continued beyond puberty it indicated to Freud a failure to grow up because of fixations or traumas in the past.

Other individuals might become "masochists," desiring punishment, often through a sense of guilt. Still others were "narcissistic," loving themselves to the exclusion of everyone else, like the beautiful youth Narcissus in the Greek myth who doted on his own image. And some persons became "exhibitionists," showing off to gain attention or to shock and so find a personal gratification.

Underneath all the terms and the descriptions of sexual development, psychoanalysis was and is basically a procedure for the investigation of mental processes inaccessible in any other way. To Freud it meant a new scientific discipline, one which he fought for strenuously and tried to hold to certain lines in the face of those who wandered off in search of new techniques. Even his long-loved friend, Ferenczi, toward the end of his life began to pursue methods which Freud could not approve; their friendship was tried but never completely broke under the strain. And when Ferenczi died in 1933, after a long illness, Freud was deeply grieved. Ferenczi, he said, took away with him a part of the old times, times of struggle and grueling effort, but times, too, of glory.

Freud himself had accomplished self-healing through his self-analysis over the years. When his daughter Anna was asked by Freud's biographer, Jones, what his outstanding characteristic was, she replied at once, "His simplicity."

Freud's physical sufferings, however, increased. Marie Bonaparte intervened, insisting that he have a regular medical attendant with him at all times. She recommended Dr. Max Schur.

Freud accepted the recommendation and at his first meeting with Schur laid down one rule; that Schur should always tell him the truth about his condition, no matter how grim it might be. He had been deeply angered by his doctors' concealing from him that the growth in his mouth was malignant. All his life he had sought the truth in every sphere, only to have his doctors out of a false kindness lie to him. He made one other stipulation to Dr. Schur. He hated sedative medicines, he said, because they dimmed his mental faculties and he wanted his mind clear. However, if the pain became greater than he could endure, he asked that the doctor not let him suffer more than necessary. Pride was important to Freud; extreme physical pain could destroy it.

So he sat among his ancient relics, his chows drowsing alongside, still writing and still pursuing the illusive shape of truth. Essays on the Russian novelist Dostoevski, or on the question of lay analyses and books continued to appear. In 1929 he published *Civilization and Its Discontents*, in which he investigated the aims of human behavior, the purpose of life and the problem of the individual in relation to society. The name of Freud had become a household word by then and within a year the book's edition of 12,000 copies was sold out. Among sophisticated circles all over, but especially in the English-speaking world, parlor conversation was filled with

Freudian analogies. "Freudian slip," "repression," "Oedipus complex," and "libido" were rapidly becoming a part of daily language. Without some knowledge of Freud, one was not really "in the know." The field of the arts, too, began to reflect his influence; painters, musicians, and artists striving to express their visions and versions of the obscure depths of the unconscious. Some persons in all walks of life misinterpreted Freud's teachings and used them as an excuse to express themselves freely, especially in sexual matters, without regard for conventional patterns or traditional morality, and Freud was unfairly blamed. As for his defenders, many were more "Freudian" than Freud and quoted Freud as if he had discovered an absolute truth.

Freud himself wrote to Romain Rolland, "Of one thing I am absolutely positive: there are certain things we cannot know now."

In July, 1930, Freud received the Goethe prize for that year, an award extremely gratifying to one who had always considered the great poet a hero of letters. Freud's address of acceptance was read by Anna.

That same month Freud's mother died at the age of ninety-five. Underneath his grief Freud experienced both a sense of freedom and relief—freedom from the worry that he might die before her and so give her anguish, relief that her own physical ordeals were over. Anna, the faithful daughter, nurse, secretary, disciple, attended the funeral in his stead.

In the meanwhile other events were taking place which were to prove crucial for the psychoanalytic movement and the uneasy political peace in the world. The crash of the stock market in the United States and the intensifying economic depression all over Europe were affecting scientists, rulers and the common people alike. Money was scarce, jobs hard to find. In Germany dissatisfied elements of the population were rallying around a fanatic Austrian determined on power, Adolf Hitler. In September, 1930, Hitler and his Nazi followers received a surprisingly large number of votes in the elections of that year. German army leaders, especially, began to wonder if Hitler was not exactly the man needed to restore the military to power and make Germany into a mighty nation again. Business leaders, bankers and finally many of the millions of unemployed Germans looked with increasing favor on the black-shirted Nazis in spite of their bullying tactics and hate-filled oratory. Humiliated by their defeat in the First World War, patriotism and hope surged up in many a German breast in response to Hitler's inflammatory speeches.

The year of 1933 found Hitler in command of the German government. On the evening of May 10, thousands of students carrying torches marched to a spot opposite the University of Berlin. There they tossed the torches onto a huge pile of books. As the books began to burn, more were thrown into the hissing flames until 20,000 volumes had been destroyed.

Among the books burned were those of Thomas Mann, Albert Einstein, H. G. Wells, André Gide, Emile Zola, Jack London—and Sigmund Freud.

In Vienna, Freud attempted to remain philosophical in the

face of the Nazi threat to culture and peace although it seemed to him that the world was turning into an enormous prison, with Germany its main cell. Nevertheless, he wrote to Eitingon about the book burning that at least the Nazis were content with burning his books instead of his person, which perhaps marked some progress over the Middle Ages.

Others were less calm, especially those Jewish analysts in Germany who felt the full force of Hitler's attempt to "liquidate" them and their psychoanalytic movement. One by one, then by twos and threes they fled the Third Reich, seeking safety and a future elsewhere. The German Society for Psychotherapy was turned into a propaganda instrument for the Nazis and it's members were ordered to study Hitler's *Mein Kampf* as the basis of their work. Carl Jung became the president of the Society. His chief function was to discriminate between Aryan psychology and Jewish psychology and to prove the superiority of the former. Not even scientific inquiry under Hitler could remain neutral. Psychoanalysis must be destroyed not only in Germany but in Austria as well.

The Nazification process began to lap across the Austrian border. Soon, many Austrians feared, Hitler's armies would follow. Freud's friends urged him to flee while there was still a chance, to go to Switzerland or America.

Freud shook his head. He refused to leave his home. Life under a dictatorship might be hard but settlement in a new country, aged and ill as he was, could be equally so. And he had duties where he was. He still treated several patients a day. He felt responsibility for his aging sisters, Rosa, Adolfine,

Marie and Paula. There was the hard-pressed publishing house to protect. His study, his consulting room and Vienna itself were his home.

He worked on, ignoring the rioting in Vienna streets, or the distant rumble and clatter of the mighty army Hitler was assembling in Germany. Operations and treatments on his jaw continued although no one, including Freud, believed that there was any longer hope of a permanent cure.

In 1936, Freud celebrated his eightieth birthday quietly, though the flat was filled with flowers and congratulations from all over. He had one chief visitor during the time, the famous German novelist, Thomas Mann. Mann had visited him before and in the meantime the association between the two had deepened.

One caller asked Freud, "How does it feel to be eighty years old?"

"The feelings of a man my age are not even a topic for conversation," Freud replied.

In September he and Martha celebrated their golden wedding anniversary with all their children present except for Oliver who was unable to be there. With a smile, Freud told Marie Bonaparte that his life with Martha "was really not a bad solution of the marriage problem."

December brought another painful operation. For the first time, Freud cried out to the surgeon Pichler, "I can't go on any longer." He went on, as he had to, pain locking his mouth so tightly that he could not eat or drink for several days.

Jofi sat sympathetically beside him, seemingly understanding everything. She herself was destined to die in the first month of 1937. Unable to get along without the comfort of a dog, Freud appealed to Dorothy Burlingham, a friend of psychoanalysis and the Freud family, to return a female chow called Lün which he had given to her four years before because of Jofi's jealousy. Dorothy Burlingham gave up the pet for Freud's sake.

In November Freud wrote to author Stefan Zweig that his work lay behind him and that he had no way of knowing how later generations would assess it. Even as he wrote, he was laboring over a final book, *Moses and Monotheism,* his mind still haunted by the statue of Michelangelo.

CHAPTER 14

The shouts of newspaper vendors shattered the usually quiet Berggasse one Saturday afternoon in 1938. Hitler's armies had begun to stream across the Austrian border the day before, March 11.

Freud commanded the maid Paula to go quickly and buy a copy of the *Abend*.

When the maid returned with the newspaper, Martin and the rest of the family watched as Freud took the paper and scanned the front page. He hoped that somehow Austria would assert its independence of the Nazis and that perhaps it was not true that Chancellor Schuschnigg had resigned. Freud fingered his glasses then suddenly crumpled the paper in his hands and flung it across the room.

The family stared in silent astonishment. Never had any of them seen the head of the household lose his self-control to such an extent. Martin unobtrusively walked over to the crumpled *Abend* and picked it up. The *Abend* had been a strong supporter of Austrian independence. Smoothing out the newspaper, he read now with shocked dismay. The paper expressed jubilance at the arrival of the Nazis. Columns were devoted to praise of Hermann Goering, Hitler's righthand man and the founder of the hated German secret police. No wonder his father had been outraged.

The next day the Austrian Nazis were in full possession of Vienna. Persecution of Jewish citizens began at once. Day after day, Jewish men and women were forced by jeering storm troopers to scrub sidewalks and gutters on their hands and knees; others were jailed and others were robbed of all their material possessions. Shouts of "Heil Hitler!" mingled with the rumble of tanks, the echoes beating against the walls at Berggasse 19.

Three days after the invasion there was a forceful knock at the door of the Freud residence. Several storm troopers pushed their way past the maid and into the dining room armed with rifles and pistols, their looks menacing. Martha reacted automatically as a hostess welcoming strangers to her house. She suggested that they rack their rifles in the umbrella stand and waving a hand toward some chairs, invited the ruffians to be seated. The soldiers looked at her blankly, confused by her hospitality.

Anna glanced nervously toward her father's study, then at her mother. Without words, they both knew what was uppermost in the other's mind. Freud, with his weak heart and other ailments, should be protected. Martha turned suddenly. When she returned, she brought with her whatever cash was in the household, placed the money on the table and told the invaders to help themselves.

The ruffians looked at her sneeringly. There was surely more money than that in the house of the famous Doktor Freud. They got up, their intent plain: they were planning to conduct their own search. In order to forestall violence and possible bloodshed Anna led the visitors toward a safe in another room and opened it. The men seized the money there ($840) and then began eyeing other possible loot in the form of art objects or furnishings.

A gaunt figure, dark eyes blazing above a trim, white beard, appeared in the doorway. Old age had not dimmed Sigmund Freud's courage, or his ability to confound cowards by the defiance in his eyes. As long ago the hecklers at Thumsee in the Tyrol had fled before his accusing stare, so now these did also. But they threatened to return.

A similar scene was being enacted at the offices of the *Verlag*. Martin Freud, who was engaged in trying to keep the company afloat, was held at gunpoint while the storm troopers helped themselves to any petty cash they could find. While they were doing this Ernest Jones arrived, having flown to Vienna when he heard of the Nazi invasion. The moment he opened his mouth in protest he was arrested, but in an hour he was released and managed to make his way to

Berggasse 19. There he urged Freud to escape the city at once, if not for his own sake for the sake of all those who cherished his life.

Freud resisted. In the first place, he said, he was too weak even to climb up into a train compartment. Also, no country would take him in as unemployed immigrants were not popular.

This was true, Jones admitted, but he was certain that he could convince the authorities in England to make an exception in Freud's case and grant him asylum.

But the Nazis might well refuse to let him leave, Freud argued. "They would prefer to keep me here where they can punish me for my misdeeds and faulty ancestry. They want their pound of flesh."

Even the Nazis wouldn't dare to strike directly at Freud, Jones insisted, for they would risk outraging the opinion of the civilized world. Freud must leave. Jones would appeal to everyone with influence, he promised, including President Franklin Roosevelt.

At last, Freud agreed to let Jones do what he could. "I think of myself now," he said, "as Jacob in the Bible who, when a very old man, was taken by his children to Egypt."

Jones left soon after, determined to make Freud's emigration to England possible. It was a hectic mission and though he was finally successful it took three months of effort, with appeals to English authorities, ambassadors of several countries, including the United States, and to the Nazi officials themselves.

Marie Bonaparte arrived in Vienna to help the Freuds prepare for the departure. She and Anna went through Freud's papers and correspondence, burning all that seemed not worth moving to London. Always the Nazi Gestapo watched and hounded the family. Martin was frequently hauled off to Gestapo headquarters for questioning. Raids on the flat were continued with the excuse that the Nazi agents were searching for political anti-Nazi documents, though they never quite gained the courage to invade Freud's own rooms.

One of the S.S. men, however, had the mistaken courage during a raid to invade Martha's linen cupboard. On his way past the cupboard he stopped, pulled its doors open and began dragging out her piles of immaculately laundered and carefully arranged linen, each package tied with colored ribbons. With the fearlessness of outrage Martha gave the man such a tongue lashing that he retreated.

On the same day that this happened the Nazis took Anna away with them to the Gestapo headquarters. Freud, pacing the floor, smoking one cigar after another, visualized the possible horror that might result. Concentration camps were already efficiently killing and torturing those whom the Nazis singled out as victims.

At seven o'clock that evening Anna reappeared at the flat, shaken but unharmed. The Nazis were still afraid to do more than follow a policy of harassment with someone as well-known as Freud and his family. Later they would be more defiant and dare to destroy millions of human beings, rich or humble, in their gas chambers and incinerators.

"Anna taken by Gestapo," Freud recorded briefly in his diary, March 22.

Through the rest of March and April the Freuds waited for the necessary exit permit which would let them go to England.

The first to be able to leave was Minna who was recuperating from an operation for cataracts on her eyes. Dorothy Burlingham personally fetched Minna from the sanatorium where she was staying and took her to London on May 5. Martin, too, and Mathilde managed to get away before their parents. Ernst was already in London.

Finally, on June 4, 1938, Freud, Martha, and Anna said farewell to the city which had been Freud's home for seventy-nine years. He had once described Vienna as being "hostile and barbarous." To most of the world it had been a symbol of gaiety, a cradle of artistic creativity. Now it had become a place of hate and confusion from which one of its most distinguished sons must flee. Behind him Freud was forced to leave his elderly sisters. They were incinerated five years later in Hitler's ovens but this, fortunately, Freud would never know.

The Orient Express went rumbling across the frontier of France at early dawn. In Paris the Freuds were met by Marie Bonaparte, Ambassador William Bullitt of the United States and Ernst. After twelve hours in Marie Bonaparte's home the party crossed by night on the ferry boat to Dover. In spite of Freud's fears about the journey he withstood it better than he had hoped, although it took several doses of nitroglycerine and strychnine to sustain the beating of his heart.

In order to avoid cameramen and reporters, Freud and his family and two maid servants arrived at a railway platform where they were not expected. Jones and his wife, and Martin and Mathilde were there to greet them. The family was taken to a London house Ernst had rented for them as a temporary refuge. On his first stroll in its garden, with its splendid view, Freud confided to Jones that he was almost tempted to exclaim, "Heil Hitler," himself, in gratitude for having been forced to such a pleasant spot.

Welcoming greetings came from all over England. So did autograph collectors, reporters and portrait painters. London papers carried stories of Freud's arrival and vied with each other in praise of his contribution to psychology. Medical journals congratulated England for having given asylum to Professor Freud.

In spite of all this, Freud's heart was torn by memories of his homeland and he wrote to Eitingon that a feeling of triumph was too strongly mingled with grief. "I always greatly loved the prison from which I have been released."

There was no refuge from the cancer eating at his jaw. Recurrences necessitated calling in medical experts. Their verdict was that nothing much more could be done. Radium treatments might, however, prolong Freud's life.

Freud had faced the thought of his own death through many years, even when he had been comparatively young. Now, living at a permanent address in London, 20 Maresfield Gardens, in September, 1938, death seemed no more alarming than his shadow as he walked through the garden with its flowers, shrubs and trees which provided him with privacy. His consulting room—he still received several patients a day —was filled with the antiquities he had managed to rescue from Vienna. Through French doors he could look out directly onto all that grew or flowered in the English autumn. Sitting there or in a swing lounge outside, Freud thought back over the years of his life, the struggles and triumphs, the friends and enemies. Some of those friends were still trying to gain the Nobel prize for him. He had told them not to waste their time. He had had rewards enough. It was a sufficient satisfaction that the International Psycho-Analytical Congress could still manage to meet, as it did in August, 1938. Anna did not dare to leave his side and so could not attend.

"I get more and more dependent on her and less on myself," he said.

The Second World War was approaching. One day there was an air-raid warning. Freud, lying on a couch in the garden looked up for a sight of German planes. Someone had said this would be the last war; it would be for him, he thought. The wail of the sirens died; it had been a false alarm.

Stoically he pursued his work and waited while cancer ate its way through to his cheek. By September of 1939 he spent most of his time on the garden couch gazing at the fading foliage. He still took no sedative drugs except an occasional aspirin to help dull his pain. On September 19 he asked Ernest Jones to come to him to say good-by. Too weak to talk he gave Jones an expressive silent wave of his hand.

Two days later he called Dr. Max Schur to him, the same doctor he had depended on in Vienna. Schur had been prevented from accompanying Freud on the flight to England by an attack of appendicitis, but had managed his escape later. Freud now reminded Schur of the pact they had once made that Schur would never let him suffer beyond the point where suffering seemed senseless. He had reached that point.

Schur pressed his hand. He had not forgotten and promised he would see to it that Freud received adequate sedation.

"Tell Anna about our talk," Freud said.

Through a mist of pain, as the hours went on, he saw and heard Anna and the other members of the family around him. Always, the figure of Martha was in the foreground. Dear Marty, still the princess to him, in spite of her own gray hair and aging face.

The next morning Schur gave Freud a third of a grain of morphia to ease his suffering. Freud gave a sigh of relief, closed his eyes and sank into a painless sleep. Close to midnight on the following day, September 23, 1939, he died.

Freud's ashes are enclosed in one of his favorite Grecian urns at Golder's Green, a suburb of London.

Of all who have attempted a scientific exploration into the depths of the human psyche, Freud has made the most permanent contribution to our understanding of our "unknown" selves. Controversy surrounds many of Freud's teachings, some persons favoring the school of Jung or Adler, others such as the neo-Freudians revising certain of Freud's doctrines in

173

the light of their own investigations. Nevertheless, it is Freud who towers over psychoanalysis like a giant, for psychoanalysis was his creation. It was he, mocked at or ignored, who first penetrated the world of dreams and saw that it had a meaning which, interpreted, could help restore many disturbed persons to a more healthful, creative life. It was he who showed that the unconscious was not a static nothingness but a dynamic, ever-present force acting on thought and action. And it was he who first emphasized that the powerful instinct bound up with reproducing human life affected not just physically mature persons but was a force operating even in infants. This theory remains the one which causes the greatest amount of controversy among people. All too often it is the only Freudian theory that the uninformed know. Yet to have a full grasp of Freud one could spend a substantial part of a lifetime studying his works and even then, find certain of his concepts difficult to understand completely. In the effort, however, one would find himself confronted with a genius who affected our era so profoundly that he changed a whole pattern of thinking, even among those who know scarcely more than his name.

In his *Autobiography*, Freud humbly expressed his own estimate of his long explorations of the human mind and spirit.

"Looking back, then, over the patchwork of my life's labours, I can say that I have made many beginnings and thrown out many suggestions. Something will come of them in the future, though I cannot myself tell whether it will be much or little. I may, however, express a hope that I have opened up a pathway for an important advance in our knowledge."

The pathway is there and all seekers after truth are bound to follow it at least part way.

CHRONOLOGICAL CALENDAR

1856 Sigmund Freud is born in Freiberg, Moravia, May 6.

1859 The Freud family moves to Leipzig.

1859 Publication of Charles Darwin's *On the Origin of Species by Means of Natural Selection.*

1860 The Freuds move to Vienna.

1861 Start of the United States Civil War.

1865 Sigmund enters Sperl Gymnasium.

1865 Gregor Mendel establishes the mechanics of heredity. Joseph Lister starts antiseptic surgery. Assassination of President Abraham Lincoln.

1866 Alexander Freud is born.

1867 Karl Marx publishes the first volume of *Das Kapital.*

1869 Sir Francis Galton applies Darwin's ideas of heredity to man's mental inheritance.

1870–71 Franco-Prussian War.

1872 Sigmund visits Fluss family in Freiberg.

1872 The *Principles of Physiological Psychology* appears, by Wilhelm Wundt, laying the groundwork for modern experimental psychology.

1873 Sigmund Freud graduates from Sperl Gymnasium in June. In Oct. he begins medical studies at the University of Vienna.

1876 In March, Freud receives a grant for zoological research in Trieste. In the fall he begins work under Ernst Brücke at the Institute of Physiology.

1880 Freud is called up for military service.

1881 Freud receives his medical degree, March 31.

1882 Freud meets Martha Bernays in April. The two become engaged, June 17. Freud decides to practice medicine and begins interning at the General Hospital of Vienna, July 31.

1884 Freud begins experiments with cocaine.

1873 The World's Fair is held in Vienna.

1875 Carl Gustav Jung and Thomas Mann are born.

1876 Alexander Graham Bell invents the telephone.

1878 Leo XIII is elected Pope.

1879 Albert Einstein is born. Thomas Alva Edison perfects the incandescent lamp.

1881 Louis Pasteur applies the principle of immunization through vaccination to rabies.

1882 Robert Koch discovers germ of tuberculosis.

1883 Diphtheria germ is identified by Edwin Klebs.

1885 In August Freud finishes his service in the General Hospital. In Oct. he goes to Paris to study under Jean M. Charcot.

1886 Freud opens his office as a practicing neurologist, April 25. On Sept. 13 he and Martha are married. He reads his paper "On Male Hysteria" to the Society of Physicians.

1887 The Sigmund Freuds' first child Mathilde is born, Oct. 16. Freud experiments in using hypnosis in treating his patients.

1889 Jean Martin Freud, a second child, is born, Dec. 6.

1891 Freud publishes a book *On Aphasia* and a lengthy monograph on paralysis in children. His third son Oliver is born, Feb. 19.

1892 Ernst Freud, the fourth child, is born, April 6. Freud

1885 Pasteur develops inoculation against hydrophobia and process of "pasteurization."

1887 Gottlieb Daimler builds first successful automobile.

1889 Adolph Hitler is born in Upper Austria.

1890 William James publishes his *Principles of Psychology*. *Laws of Imitation* by Gabriel de Tarde published, important work in field of social psychology.

uses "psychical analysis" on a patient for the first time.

1893 The Freuds' fifth child, Sophie, is born, April 12.

1894 Serum for diphtheria is developed by Emil von Behring.

1895 Freud and Breuer publish *Studies on Hysteria*. Freud makes the first complete analysis of one of his own dreams. Anna Freud, his sixth and last child, is born, Dec. 3.

1895 William Roentgen detects X-rays. Guglielmo Marconi invents wireless telegraphy.

1896 Freud's father dies, Oct. 23.

1897 Freud begins an intensive self analysis in July and continues his researches into the meaning of dreams.

1898 Pierre and Marie Curie isolate radium. Spanish-American War

1899 *The Interpretation of Dreams* is published, November.

1899 South African Boer War

1900 Max Planck propounds the quantum theory. Boxer Rebellion in China

1901 Death of British Queen Victoria.

1902 The first psychoanalytic society meets at Freud's house. Freud secures the title of Associate Professor at the University of Vienna.

1903 Wright brothers make first successful airplane flight.

1905 Freud publishes *The Psychopathology of Everyday Life; Jokes and Their Connection with the Unconscious; Three Essays on the Theory of Sexuality.*

1905 Einstein sets forth a special theory on relativity which gives a new turn to research on the atom.

1906 Freud begins corresponding with Jung.

1908 The first International Psycho-Analytical Congress meets in Salzburg, April 26.

1909 Freud makes a trip to the United States to give a lecture course at Clark University.

1910 Beginning and growth of the psychoanalytical movement. In March, the 2nd International Congress takes place. Freud's *A General Introduction to Psycho-Analysis* is published.

1912 Frederick Soddy shows the existence of isotopes.

1913 Freud and Jung part company. A group of followers loyal to Freud's theories band together around him as the Committee.

1914 The assassination of the Archduke Francis Ferdinand of Austria, June 28, precipitates World War I.

1916 Death of Emperor Franz Joseph.

1917 Bolshevik Revolution in Russia, November 6. United States declares war on Germany.

1918 Collapse of the Austro-Hungarian Empire. End of World War I, November 11.

1919 The publishing house, the *Internationaler Psychoanalytischer Verlag*, is founded.

1919 The signing of the Treaty of Versailles.

1920 The Berlin Policlinic, training center for analysts, opens. Daughter Sophie dies, January.

1920 The League of Nations is founded. Ernest Rutherford proposes a method for artificial disintegration of the atom.

1923 Freud has the first of many jaw operations. Publishes *The Ego and the Id*.

1927 Freud publishes *The Future of an Illusion.*

1929 Freud publishes *Civilization and Its Discontents.*

1930 Freud receives the Goethe Prize, July. His mother dies, September 12.

1936 Sigmund and Martha Freud celebrate their golden wedding anniversary, September 13.

1938 Freud, Martha and Anna leave Vienna for England, June.

1939 Freud dies in London, September 23. His *Moses and Monotheism* is published.

1927 Charles A. Lindbergh makes the first non-stop solo transatlantic flight.

1929 The stock market collapses in the United States.

1930 Ninth planet, Pluto, located.

1933 Hitler comes to power in Germany.

1936 Spanish Civil War breaks out. Abdication of Edward VIII in England.

1938 The Nazis invade Austria, March 11.

1939 In March, Germany occupies Bohemia and Moravia and invades Poland, Sept. 1. England and France declare war on Germany, Sept. 3. World War II is under way.

GLOSSARY

ANXIETY—a form of fear, especially of imaginary dangers. Persistent anxiety may occur as a reaction against fears or strong desires hidden in one's unconscious, in which case it becomes an anxiety neurosis.

APHASIA—the loss of the ability to speak clearly or to understand the speech of others.

ASSOCIATION—a linking together, as when a word makes one think of another (chicken; egg) or a memory calls up a second memory. The way a person associates words, acts, symbols or memories can provide a valuable clue to inner mental life.

BLOCK—a mental-emotional wall which stands in the way of a person's ability to act, reason or feel spontaneously.

CATHARSIS—an emptying out, as when one is "drained" of emotion or thought. In psychoanalysis, the elimination of a complex by bringing it to consciousness where it can be expressed.

DEMENTIA PRAECOX—the term first applied to schizophrenia. A form of mental disease usually developing in adolescence, in which the individual loses interest in life, people and things, and shows a gradual disintegration of personality.

DREAMS—to Freud, dreams are the life of the sleeping mind and hold the key to studying the unconscious through means of dream symbols; no dream is meaningless and its essential function is the fulfillment of a wish.

Latent Dream Thoughts—the hidden features of a dream buried beneath the dream's surface structure.

Manifest Dream Thoughts—the surface part of the dream.

EGO—the self or the "I" of the individual which, according to

Freud, has the task of self preservation. Its job is to select or regulate the demands of the basic instincts contained in the id and to try to exclude those instinctual desires which conflict with external reality.

EROS—the Greek god of love. To Freud, Eros represents the love instinct striving for self preservation and the preservation of human life as against the destructive instincts in human beings.

EXHIBITIONISM—a self-satisfied display or showing off to attract attention to oneself; among sexual deviants, exposure of the sex organs.

FIXATION—in ordinary psychological terms, the formation of a habit or association. In psychoanalysis, a condition in which the psyche is "fixed" or arrested at a certain stage. A person whose development toward maturity was arrested by too strong an attachment to a parent would be said to have a mother or father fixation.

FREE ASSOCIATION—a technique in psychoanalysis in which the patient is encouraged to let his thoughts drift freely and to speak whatever comes into his mind.

FREUDIAN SLIP—occurs when one says or writes something other than what he intended to, revealing what he secretly thinks or feels.

FRUSTRATION—a state of being denied satisfaction of a desire or wish; the desire may be unconscious. To Freud, frustration means generally the lack of a satisfactory sexual outlet, precipitating neurosis.

HALLUCINATION—hearing, seeing or feeling things that do not actually exist; usually arising from a disorder of the nervous system or mental illness.

HYPNOSIS—a process of putting a person into a trance or partial sleep. A hypnotized person is responsive to suggestions and commands made to him by the hypnotist, to varying degrees. Not all persons can be hypnotized.

HYPOCHONDRIAC—one who suffers morbid anxiety over health, imagining that every ache or pain means he has a serious illness.

HYSTERIA—a form of mental disturbance. A hysterical patient often turns his emotional conflicts into physical symptoms (conversion hysteria) so that he "imagines" that he is blind, deaf, suffocating or paralyzed.

ID—the storehouse of the instincts, entirely in the unconscious, containing all that is inherited; the seat of blind, pleasure-seeking energy, knowing neither past nor future, good nor evil.

INHIBITION—the inability to do something one may want to do either through conscious or unconscious fear of the result. A "brake" on the ability of the ego to express itself freely.

INSTINCT—an inborn, inherited force as in the drive toward satisfying hunger, mating and reproducing one's kind or avoiding danger.

LATENCY PERIOD—the time of life from about age four to the start of mature physical development, or puberty, around age eleven.

LIBIDO—the sex drive or love instinct; energy and desire derived from the sex instinct or from the primal urge to live.

MASOCHISM—taking pleasure in being hurt or abused; medically, pleasure in receiving sexual abuse, and therefore a perversion.

NARCISSISM—exaggerated self love and concern. The name comes from the Greek legend of a boy, Narcissus, who fell in love with his own reflected image.

NEURASTHENIA—nervous weakness or exhaustion; one of the milder forms of mental illness, usually with symptoms of extreme tiredness and an inability to cope with the common stresses of life.

NEUROLOGIST—a specialist in diseases of the nervous system.

NEUROSIS—a comparatively mild form of psychic disturbance, often resulting from inner conflicts in childhood; a breakdown in the ability of the ego to cope with the outer world in the face of the demands of the inner, instinctual drives. Neuroses take various forms: anxiety, hysteria, extreme nervousness, a general inability to meet the demands of a job or of human relationships. Many persons are somewhat neurotic but are able to handle their lives reasonably well in spite of this.

OEDIPUS COMPLEX—a stage of development of a boy, between age five and seven, when he wants to replace his father in his mother's affections. Girls going through the same stage of rivalry with the mother are said to have an Electra complex. If we say an adult has an Oedipus complex, as when a grown man remains in an immature relationship to or dependence on his mother, we mean that he has not developed beyond the Oedipal stage.

PHOBIA—an exaggerated fear of certain objects or conditions; as of heights, being alone, snakes, travel, caves, etc.

PLEASURE PRINCIPLE—avoidance of pain, the main governing force of the id.

PROJECTION—the blaming of others for one's own mistakes or failures.

PSYCHE—from the Greek word meaning soul. The mind; mental life.

PSYCHIATRY—a *medical* science limited to disorders of mind and emotion and their treatment, both psychoses and neuroses, and frequently involving use of drugs, shock treatment, occupational therapy and the like. All psychiatrists have medical degrees.

PSYCHOANALYSIS—a method, originated by Freud, of treating certain forms of mental illness by encouraging the patient to recall and describe repressed memories and emotions in order to bring them to consciousness. It is also an accumulation of knowledge about, and a theory of human behavior, as well as a means of investigating and increasing psychological knowledge.

PSYCHOLOGY—the scientific study of mental processes and behavior; intelligence, learning ability, education, memory, emotions, etc. Not confined to mental illness alone.

PSYCHOSIS—severe mental illness, commonly called "insanity."

PSYCHOSOMATIC—the interrelationship between mind and body and the way they affect each other. Psychosomatic medicine treats disorders that are brought on by mental or emotional disturbance.

PSYCHOTHERAPY—a psychological form of therapy for mental illness, relying mostly on verbal communication (talks, probing for motives and self-understanding) rather than on drugs or other physical methods. A social worker, a minister or a psychiatrist may use psychotherapy in their work. Psychoanalysis is one specialized form of psychotherapy.

RATIONALIZATION—inability or unwillingness to see or admit to the actual causes of one's behavior and attitudes; blaming the wrong reason for one's acts as a way of not facing the true cause.

REALITY PRINCIPLE—opposite of the pleasure principle, reality being the facts and conditions presented by the outside world.

REGRESSION—an unconsciously motivated psychological mechanism in which a person goes back to earlier childish types of behavior, as to childish weeping or tantrums; the return of the libido to earlier stages of development or to infantile attachments.

REPRESSION—the "burying" of painful desires and memories in the unconscious, especially those which would cause intense conflict if brought to consciousness; however, the suppressed desires remain dynamic and affect behavior, constantly seeking an outlet.

RESISTANCE—in psychoanalysis, the patient's fighting against the analyst's attempts to make him aware of unconscious motivations. Overcoming this inner opposition is one of the psychoanalyst's main problems, part of the reason why a complete analysis almost always takes a long time.

SADISM—pleasure in inflicting pain on others. Medically, a sexual perversion in which satisfaction is gained by abusing a loved one.

SCHIZOPHRENIA—a severe mental disorder in which a patient loses contact with reality through growing disinterest, withdrawal into himself, an emotional sluggishness, with a gradual fragmenting of his personality. Paranoid schizophrenics suffer delusions of being persecuted, or may imagine that they are great figures such as Napoleon.

SIBLINGS—children in the same family.

SUBCONSCIOUS—not present in the conscious, or operating at the lowest margin of consciousness. This term is not used by Freud.

SUBLIMATION—channeling sexual energy away from a sexual object into other spheres such as social service, artistic creation, scientific discovery, sports, etc.

SUPEREGO—the conscience or "inner voice" which acts as a judge instructing the individual as to right and wrong. It controls the ego and is responsible for feelings of guilt and anxiety. The superego echoes early teachings of parents and other persons in authority.

SYMBOL—that which suggests or represents something else to which it is related or associated. Where certain desires are repressed in the unconscious, they find expression through symbols or symbolic acts which the ego finds acceptable. Phallic symbols represent the reproductive organs.

TRANSFERENCE—a situation in which a patient under analysis identifies his analyst with some important figure in his life, often one important in his childhood, such as a parent, and passes on to the analyst the feelings he has for that person. The patient's feeling toward the analyst can be affectionate or hostile. The success of the analysis depends on the quality of the transference and the analyst's ability to interpret it and use it to help the patient understand himself.

TRAUMA—a physical trauma is an injury to the body. A psychic trauma is a shock or blow to the emotions.

UNCONSCIOUS—any mental process of which one is not aware; that part of the psyche beneath the level of consciousness which contains repressed desires and the ideas associated with them, but which exerts a continuing influence on what we think, feel and do.

WISH FULFILLMENT—the satisfaction of unrealized desires and even unknown wishes through fantasy or through dreams in which one pictures a situation he would like to have exist in actual life. Wish fulfillment can be at work also (though not always) in a seemingly contradictory way as when a person says of someone he deeply dislikes, "I hope nothing terrible happens to him," suggesting that he unconsciously wishes something terrible *would* happen.

SELECTED BIBLIOGRAPHY

BRILL, A. A. *Psychoanalytic Psychiatry.* New York: Knopf, 1946.

FREUD, MARTIN. *Sigmund Freud: Man and Father.* New York: Vanguard, 1959.

FREUD, SIGMUND. *An Autobiographical Study.* Translated by JAMES STRACHEY. New York: Norton, 1963.

―――― *Basic Writings of Sigmund Freud.* Translated and edited by A. A. BRILL. New York: Random House, 1939.

―――― *Beyond the Pleasure Principle.* New York: Bantam by arrangement with Liveright, 1959.

―――― *Delusion and Dream.* Boston: Beacon by arrangement with Dodd Mead, 1956.

―――― *Dictionary of Psychoanalysis,* eds. NANDOR FODOR and FRANK GAYNOR. New York: Philosophical Library, 1958.

―――― *Dora—An Analysis of a Case of Hysteria.* Riverside, N.J.: Collier by arrangement with Basic Books, 1963.

―――― *The Ego and the Id.* Translated by JAMES STRACHEY. New York: Norton, 1962.

―――― *A General Introduction to Psychoanalysis.* Translated by JOAN RIVIERE. New York: Pocket Books by arrangement with Liveright, 1953.

―――― *The Interpretation of Dreams.* Translated and edited by JAMES STRACHEY. New York: John Wiley by arrangement with Basic Books, 1961.

―――― *Letters,* ed. ERNST FREUD, translated by JAMES and TANIA STERN. New York: Basic Books, 1960.

―――― *The Origins of Psychoanalysis* (*Letters to Wilhelm Fliess*), ed. MARIE BONAPARTE *et al.* New York: Basic Books, 1954.

FREUD, SIGMUND. *Totem and Taboo.* New York: Random House by arrangement with A. A. BRILL, 1963.

FROMM, ERICH. *Sigmund Freud's Mission.* New York: Harper, 1959.

JONES, ERNEST. *The Life and Work of Sigmund Freud.* 3 vols. New York: Basic Books, 1953, 1955, 1957.

NELSON, BENJAMIN (ed.). *Freud and the 20th Century.* Cleveland: World, 1957.

SACHS, HANNS. *Freud: Master and Friend.* London: Imago, 1945.

SCHOENWALD, RICHARD L. *Freud: The Man and His Mind, 1856–1956.* New York: Knopf, 1956.

ACKNOWLEDGMENTS

For permission to quote, grateful acknowledgment is made to Basic Books, Inc., George Allen and Unwin Ltd., The Hogarth Press Ltd. and Vanguard Press, Inc.

From *The Interpretation of Dreams* by Sigmund Freud. New York: Basic Books, 1961 and London: George Allen and Unwin Ltd.

From *The Letters of Sigmund Freud,* edited by Ernst L. Freud. New York: Basic Books, 1960 and London: The Hogarth Press Ltd.

From *The Life and Work of Sigmund Freud* by Ernest Jones. New York: Basic Books, 1953, 1955, 1957.

From *The Origins of Psychoanalysis: Sigmund Freud's Letters to Wilhelm Fleiss,* edited by Marie Bonaparte and others. Basic Books: New York, 1954.

From *Sigmund Freud: Man and Father* by Martin Freud. New York: Vanguard Press, 1959.

For the use of the frontispiece photograph, grateful acknowledgment is made to Ernst L. Freud.

INDEX

Abraham, Karl, 122, 130, 133, 137, 138
  antagonism between Carl Jung and, 124
  death, 153
Adler, Alfred, 115, 124, 130, 173
  Freudian ranks deserted by, 129, 133
  new techniques developed by, 145
  resentment of Jung by, 129
analyst, lay, 144–145, 154
analytic technique, importance of, 145
Andreas-Salomé, Lou, 137, 141
Aphasia, 77–78
Autobiography, 127, 174–175

Berlin Policlinic, 142
Bernays, Anna, 95

Bernays, Eli, 35, 36, 39, 40, 48, 50, 51, 56, 95
  engaged to Anna Freud, 52
  financial help from, 138–139
  married to Anna Freud, 63
Bernays, Frau, 36, 41, 44–45, 52, 56, 57
Bernays, Martha, 40–42, 44–49, 50, 51, 57, 58, 60, 61–64, 70, 71
  See also Freud, Martha
Bernays, Minna, 35, 36, 40, 41, 48, 52, 56, 60, 62, 70, 75, 91, 92, 97, 113, 170
biographer, Freud's. *See* Jones, Ernest
Bleuler, Eugene, 121, 124, 152
Bonaparte, Princess Marie, 141, 155, 158–159, 163, 169, 170
book-burning, Berlin, 161, 162

Brandes, George, 152
Breuer, Josef, 34, 53–55, 59, 60, 70, 75, 77, 82, 84–85, 87, 88, 113, 153, 156
Breuer, Mathilde, 54, 70, 75
Brill, A. A., 122, 154
Brücke, Ernst, 29–31, 33, 34–35, 43–44, 61
Bullit, Ambassador William, 170
Burghölzli Clinic of Psychiatry. *See* clinics
Burlingham, Dorothy, 164, 170

"Case of Anna O., The," 85, 156
Charcot, Jean M., 62, 63, 65–69
Civilization and Its Discontents, 159
Clark University, Worcester, Mass., 125
clinics, psychiatric, 55, 70, 121
Committee, the, 133, 140, 153
complexes, 129, 157, 160

Darwin, Charles, 25, 153
death wish, 131, 144
desires, repressed, 109–112
Dora, case history of, 116–120
dream-analysis, 89–90, 96, 99–101, 118–119, 174
dreams, theory of. *See* wish-fulfillment theory

ego, 147–148
Ego and the Id, The, 147
Einstein, Albert, 152–153, 161

Eitingon, Max, 122, 123, 133, 162, 171
Exner, Sigmund, 30, 35, 43

Ferenczi, Sandor, 122, 124, 125–126, 130, 133, 137
death, 158
stopped from reading paper on Freudian theory, 132
Verlag director, 142
Ferstel, Baron and Baroness, 121
"fixation," 157
Fleischl-Marxow, Ernst von, 30, 31–32, 33, 35, 43, 58–60, 153
Fliess, Dr. Wilhelm, 86–87, 92–93, 95–96, 101
Freud's waning friendship with, 113
Fluss family, 21–25
Emil, 33
Gisela, 17, 34
Richard, 33, 37
Fragment of an Analysis of a Case of Hysteria, 120
Fraulein Elizabeth (von R.), early patient of Freud, 79–80
"free association," 118, 156
Freud, Adolfine, 12, 95, 162
Freud, Alexander, 8, 12, 13, 16–18, 43, 50, 95, 114
Freud, Amalie, 7, 8, 9, 10, 17, 20, 27, 61, 64, 100–101, 137, 138
death, 160

Freud, Anna (sister of Sigmund Freud), 9, 12, 13, 17, 35, 39, 51
  engaged to Eli Bernays, 52
  married, 63
Freud, Anna (daughter of Sigmund Freud), 82, 91, 96, 98, 104, 125, 135–137, 146–147, 148, 152, 154, 158, 160, 166–167, 170, 172, 173
  interest of, in her father's work, 134, 140, 141
  nurse and companion of her father, 149–150
  taken by Gestapo, 169–170
Freud, Emmanuel, 8, 20–21, 27
  death, 136–137
Freud, Ernst, 82, 134, 137, 170, 171
  Berlin Policlinic building designed by, 142
Freud, Jakob, 7, 8, 9, 10, 11, 12, 27
  death, 92–93
Freud, John, 20, 21
Freud, Julius, 8, 61, 131
Freud, Marie, 12, 39, 163
Freud, Martha, 71, 74, 75, 81, 82, 83, 104, 105, 113, 123, 125, 135, 138, 141, 145, 146–147, 152, 155, 156, 163, 166–167, 170, 173
  Nazis confronted by, 169
Freud, Martin, 81, 98, 104–106, 134, 136, 165–166, 169, 171

efforts of, to save the *Verlag*, 143, 167
escape of, from Nazi persecution, 170, 171
marriage, 140
Freud, Mathilde, 97, 98, 125
  birth, 75
  illness of, 82–83
  marriage to Robert Hollitscher, 134
  See also Hollitscher, Mathilde
Freud, Oliver, 81, 104, 105–106, 134, 137, 142, 163
Freud, Paula, 12, 95, 163
Freud, Pauline, 27
Freud, Philipp, 8, 20, 27, 101
Freud, Rosa, 12, 17, 38, 162
Freud, Sigmund
  anxieties, unreasonable, 71, 84, 87, 101
  aphasia, study of, 77–78
  awareness of anti-Semitism, 11, 21, 103, 105–107, 150
  birth, 8
  birthdays
    eightieth, 163
    seventieth, 152–154
    sixty-eighth, 150
  birthplace, 16, 21
  B'nai B'rith membership, 103, 153
  at Brücke Institute of Physiology, 29–33, 33–35, 43
  children, 75, 81, 82, 98, 104

Freud, Sigmund (*continued*)
  cocaine experiments, 58–60
  collaboration with Breuer, 84–85
  correspondence with colleagues, 137
  correspondence with Martha Bernays, 45–46, 47, 48–49, 56–57, 68–69,
  courtship, 40–42
  death, 173
  dogs, 155, 159, 163–164
  engagement, 44, 46, 52
  fainting fits, 131
  family responsibilities, 43, 56, 64, 95
    as a father, 82–83, 104
  father's attitude toward, 9–11, 14, 27
  favoritism, family, toward, 7–15, 39, 61
  filial attitude
    toward father, 7–15, 21, 23, 31, 61, 92–93, 95, 102
    toward mother, 92, 101, 102, 138, 160
  finances, 32, 42–43, 44, 56, 60, 70, 75, 84, 89, 95, 138–139
  financial relations with Breuer, 35, 60, 88, 89
  flight from Vienna, 170–171
  foreign travels, 65–69, 99, 113–115, 125–127, 148
  Freiberg visit, 16–24
  girl-consciousness, first, 22–24

Goethe prize won by, 160
golden wedding anniversary, 163
graduation from Sperl Gymnasium, 25
humor, 18, 36, 57
internship, 47
jealousy, capacity for, 39, 41–42, 45, 71
knowledge of languages, 25–26, 139
lectures by, 86, 125
marriage, 70–71
medical practice, qualifying for, 26, 33, 43, 52, 55, 58, 61
military service, 32, 70
moods, 18, 34, 86
mother's extreme devotion to, 7–8, 10, 18, 27, 92, 101
nervous disorders, interest in, 58, 62, 63, 66, 68, 76–77, 79
nervousness of, preceding train trips, 18–19, 71, 84, 120
neurologist, 62, 70–90, 103
Oedipus Rex, significant to, 60–61, 102
operations on, for cancer, 146–147, 148–150, 154, 163
opposition to, 74, 129–130, 132–133
orthodox Hebrew ritual, anathema to, 44, 63, 153
persecution by Nazis, 166–170
physical ailments, 18, 27–28, 46–47, 94, 138, 145–173

physical appearance, 8, 64, 123
postgraduate traveling grant
won by, 61
psychiatric training, 55
psychiatry, early interest in, 51
psychopathology, interest in,
69
recognition, 121–127, 134, 150,
159–160
research work, 27, 29–33, 43,
70, 74, 141
scholastic achievements, 25–
26, 27
self-analysis, 93, 95–96, 97, 98–
99, 102, 104, 120, 158
self-appraisal, 69, 86–87
self-torment, capacity for, 41,
46–47
smoking habits, 32, 64, 87, 138,
145–146
theories of, regarding sex instinct, 77, 85, 103, 116–117,
132, 144, 174
vacations with family, 89, 96–
98, 104–107
writings, 78, 85, 88, 90, 99,
104, 108, 112, 114, 115, 116,
120, 122, 126, 127, 128, 141,
143, 147, 159, 164, 174–175
youth, 7–28
Freud, Sophie, 82, 96–97, 135
engagement to Max Halber-
stadt, 134
See also Halberstadt,
Sophie

"Freud Group," 123
"Freudian Age," 112
Freudian slips, 115–116, 132, 160
Freund, Anton von, 141
Verlag director, 142

General Introduction to Psycho-
Analysis, A, 126
Gide, André, 161
Goethe, Freud's interest in, 14–
15, 25
Goering, Hermann, 166
Gross, Otto, 121
Guilbert, Yvette, 152
guilts, secret, 80
See also unconscious, the

Hajek, Dr., 146
Halberstadt, Heinerle, 145
death, 147
Halberstadt, Max, 142
engagement to Sophie Freud,
134
Halberstadt, Sophie
children, 140, 145, 147
death, 141–142
See also Freud, Sophie
Hall, Stanley, 125
Hitler, Adolf, 82, 104, 161–163,
165–166
Hollitscher, Mathilde, 142, 145,
170, 171
See also Freud, Mathilde
Hollitscher, Robert, 142
marriage to Mathilde Freud,
134

human behavior, hidden motivations of, 55, 71, 84
hypnosis, 53, 54–55, 62, 67, 70, 71–72, 75, 76, 91
hysteria, 53–55, 62, 67, 72–74, 77, 85, 95, 120

"id," 147–148
Internationaler Psychoanalytischer Verlag, 142–143, 155, 167
Interpretation of Dreams, The, 90, 108, 112, 122

James, William, 127
Jones, Ernest, 112, 122, 123, 124, 125, 130, 133, 137, 139, 171, 172
  resignation from neurological appointment because of following Freud's methods, 132
  Freud's escape from Nazi persecution aided by, 167–168
Jung, Carl G., 121–122, 123, 128–132, 173
  antagonism between Karl Abraham and, 124
  President of German Society for Psychotherapy, 162
  psychoanalytical periodical edited by, 124
  new techniques developed by, 145
  rift with Freud, 128–132, 133

Kahane, Max, 115
Kassowitz Children's Institute, 70, 78
Koller, Carl, 59
Krafft-Ebing, Richard von, 91

lay analyst, 144–145, 154
libido, 116–117, 128, 160
London, Jack, 161

Male Hysteria, On, lecture by Freud, 72
Mann, Thomas, 161, 163
Mayer, Max, 41, 45
memories, buried, 77, 80
  forgotten, 77, 79, 80, 93, 99
  unconscious, 93
  See also unconscious, the
mental disorders, treatment of, 69, 70
  approach to problem of, 78
Meynert, Dr. Theodor, 51–52, 72–73, 78
Meynert's Psychiatric Clinic. *See* clinics
Moses and Monotheism, 114

Nazis, 143, 161–163, 165–169
Neo-Freudians, 173–174
Neuroses attributed to sexual disturbance, 77, 87, 90–91, 95, 144
Nothnagel, Dr. Hermann, 51–52

Paneth, Josef, 63
Pappenheim, Bertha, 53, 75, 77, 85
  See also "Case of Anna O., The"
Pfister, Oskar, 130, 132
Physiology, Brücke Institute of, 29–33
Pichler, Professor Hans, 149, 163
"pleasure principle," 143, 144
psychiatry. See psychoanalysis
"psychical analysis," 79–80
psychoanalysis, 88, 91, 99, 121, 122, 123, 129, 132–134, 135, 137, 142, 144, 154, 155, 158, 174
Psycho-Analytic Association, 128–129
Psycho-Analytical Association
  Fifth Congress of, 138
  Jung's resignation from, 132
Psycho-Analytical Association, International, 140
Psycho-Analytical Congress, International, 123–124, 172
"Psychological Wednesday Society," 115, 122
psychology, new approach to, 78, 87
Psychology of Dementia Praecox, The, 122
Psychopathology of Everyday Life, The, 115, 126
Psychotherapy, German Society for, 162

psychosis, 148
Putnam, Dr. James, 137

Rank, Otto, 130, 133, 137, 148, 154
  Verlag director, 142–143
"reality principle," 143, 144
Reik, Theodor, 142, 154
Reitler, Rudolf, 115
"repression," 160
Ring Theatre fire, 37
rings, given to Committee members, 133, 140–141
Rolland, Romain, 150, 152, 160

Sachs, Hanns, 130 133, 137, 142
Salpêtrière, charity Hospital of, 65–66
Schönberg, Ignaz, 35, 36, 37, 40, 52, 56, 62
  death, 69–70
Schur, Dr. Max, 159, 173
Sekundararzt, 55
sex instinct, Freud's theories on, 54, 60–61, 77, 79, 85–87, 90–91, 95, 102–103, 110, 111–112, 116–120, 128–130, 132, 144, 157–158, 160, 174
Silberstein, 19
sisters, Freud's, killed by Nazis, 170
Society of Physicians, 72, 74
Society of Psychiatry and Neurology, 91

Sperl Gymnasium, 9, 22, 25
Stekel, Wilhelm, 115
Studies on Hysteria, collaboration between Breuer and Freud, 85
sublimation, 117
suggestion, power of, 76
"super-ego," 148
Supplements to the Theory of Dreams, 143
Symbols of the Libido, 128

talking method, 53–54, 75, 76, 91, 156
theories, Adler's and Jung's, 131
theories, Freudian, 143–144, 173–174
  indignation at, 116–117, 132–133
  opposition to, 129–130, 132–133
Three Essays on the Theory of Sexuality, 116
"transference," 156–157

Trieste experimental station, 27–28, 30

unconscious, the, 85, 99, 109–110, 112, 118, 119, 128, 156, 174

Vienna
  Academy of Sciences of, 31
  General Hospital of, 47–62
  University of, 26, 52, 138
Vienna Psycho-Analytical Society, 122
Verlag, See *Internationaler Psychoanalytischer Verlag*

Wahle, Fritz, 41, 45
Wells, H. G., 161
wish-fulfillment theory, 90, 98, 109–112, 143
World War, I, 134–138, 161
World War II, 172

Zola, Emile, 161
Zweig, Stefan, 150, 164

ABOUT THE AUTHORS

Adrien Stoutenburg and Laura Nelson Baker have collaborated on a number of fine books for young people, including *Scannon: Dog with Lewis and Clark* and biographies of Snowshoe Thompson, David Douglas, Carl Linnaeus and Olivia Langdon Clemens, Mark Twain's wife.

Miss Stoutenburg is a native of Minnesota where she attended the Minneapolis School of Arts. Her poetry has appeared in many national magazines and *Heroes, Advise Us,* her first volume of poetry, received the Lamont Poetry Prize in 1964.

Mrs. Baker was born in Iowa and studied at the University of Minnesota. For several years she was the editor of a weekly newspaper in a Minneapolis suburb and in 1953 won the Women's National Press Club award in the weekly editorial classification.

The authors live now in Lagunitas, California.